On a Hill above a Valley
A Teenager's War

To Joan.

Best Wishes from

Violet Butler.

The Navy, Army and Air Force Institutes

SERVITOR SERVIENTIUM

has directed that this Memorial be presented to

Violet Winifred Mary Chandler

as a formal testimony to the endurance, courage and devotion with which, under exceptional conditions of strain, hardship and danger, she unfailingly performed her duties to the Corporation in its task of serving His Majesty's Forces in the Dover area during the period of intensive bombardment by the guns of the enemy from across the Channel following the invasion of North West Europe by the Allies in June, 1944.

J. H. Crosier

Secretary.

1: The Memorial Certificate presented to the Author

On a Hill above a Valley
A Teenager's War

by

VIOLET BUTLER

Buckland Publications Limited
Barwick Road, Dover, Kent CT17 0LG

First Published 2001

ISBN 0 7212 0952 1

Printed and bound in Great Britain by
Buckland Press Ltd., Dover, Kent.

CONTENTS

LIST OF ILLUSTRATIONS

Page Number

ODE TO LORDS FIELD

What are they thinking, tomorrow's men,
As clear of eye, and straight
They gaze at chef, with ladle poised,
Across the steel hotplate?
What's for breakfast, skilley again,
And fried eggs, half congealed?
. . . The bombers were over again last night?
But fear must be concealed.

What's for dinner? Shepherd's pie, and for pudding?
Carrot flan? Will there be second helpings?
I wonder, how's my gran?
I'd break out and see mother and poor old Rover,
But it's 'six of the best', and bending over.

What's for tea? Bread and jam?
It was fruit cake on Sunday,
Why didn't they come? Don't they know
It's the one day when each word is treasured,
And hours pass so quickly, time that cannot be measured?

What's for supper? Just gravy poured over bread?
Not much for a chap on his way to bed,
Cor, look over there, Mike, the sky's all alight.
Oh! God, keep my family safe tonight.

What are they thinking, the men of today,
Rememb'ring how they were then?
Seeing the boys at the football match
Fenced like animals in a pen.
Do they think of the fears of their formative years,
Or thank God they were young way-back-when?

Violet Butler

ACKNOWLEDGMENTS

On a hill above a valley
Stands a camp, a lovely camp,
Where Southampton boys are sheltered
From the cold, and from the damp.

So, to the tune of *Darling Clementine*, sang the hundreds of boys who were evacuated to Lords Field camp, Overton, during the war years.

This book recalls those days when the boys, under strict supervision, spent their schooldays in the quiet countryside, while, thirty miles away in Southampton, their parents and families were subjected to heavy bombing.

Personal memories, too, of work and leisure, both in Hampshire and 'Hellfire Corner'.

I gratefully acknowledge the help given by the former evacuees and their relatives, especially:

Colin Douglas,	Burton on Trent, Staffs	
Barrington Little	Bitterne, Southampton	Dormitory 3
David W. Hampton	Woolston, Southampton	Dormitory 2
William Lynn	Swaythling, Southampton	
Donald Mason	Swansea, South Wales	
Robert Flather	Norwich, Norfolk	Dormitory 4
Kenneth Jack	Woolston, Southampton	
Paul Reader	Swaythling, Southampton	
Michael Parker	Woolston, Southampton	
Peter Wright	Swaythling, Southampton	

James Warren	Reading, Berkshire
G. Bourne,	Fareham, Hants
Mrs Elsie Mason	Lordshill, Southampton
Mrs D. Lovegrove	Basingstoke, Hants
Mrs Jean Wilson	Alton, Hants
Mrs Dorothy Ward	Swaythling, Southampton
Mrs May Davies	Woolston, Southampton

and to all who sent copies of the *Southern Echo* to the widely dispersed ex-pupils of Lords Field camp

Chapter One

INTRODUCTION TO LORDS FIELD

THE HAZY AUTUMN MIST which had shrouded the sea and obscured the fine old Norman castle was beginning to clear as I prepared to leave that part of England which had earned the name Hellfire Corner. I had said goodbye to my father before he had left for work an hour or so previously and now, carrying a small suitcase apiece and the inevitable gas-mask, my mother and I set out for the railway station.

It was October, 1940, and the battle of Britain was at its height; the night had been fairly quiet, allowing us the luxury of a good night's sleep, but now a lone German airman, taking advantage of the rapidly clearing sky, appeared as if from nowhere, expertly guiding his glinting craft to resume the daily machine-gun attacks on the twenty or so barrage balloons which hovered at strategic points above and around the town. The sirens wailed and grey and white puffs of exploding anti-aircraft shells marred the ever increasing blue of the sunny autumn sky, near, but not near enough, to bring down the plane, which, despite its dull khaki camouflage, shone like an elusive silver moth as its perspex dome reflected the sun's rays.

We had already passed the air-raid shelter on the quaintly named Noah's Ark Road and, laden as we were, scuttled down the hill, thankfully diving into the pillared doorway of the local Co-op. Apart from the fairly remote possibility of stopping a stray spent machine-gun shellcase, or being hit by shrapnel from the ack-ack shellbursts, there was no real danger, as we knew only too well from experience that the German pilot would concentrate only on clearing the skies of the barrage balloons in preparation for the waves of aircraft which were almost certain to follow later in the day, and which were equally certain to be intercepted by the 'famous few' of our own air force in the dogfights which we had come to regard as almost commonplace.

The balloons, too, with few exceptions, burned themselves out before the last shreds of blackened silver fabric drifted to the ground but, having allowed plenty of time in anticipation of such interruptions, we waited until the lone gunner had deftly potted his last target before continuing on our journey

'Cheeky devil,' said a woman from a nearby doorway, 'Do you know it costs £200 every time one o' them balloons gets shot down?' Local opinion as to the cost of replacing the aforementioned balloons varied from £50 to £500; with a word or two of condemnation of the 'cheeky devil' and an apprehensive glance skywards, we set out on the remaining half of our journey. Taxis, even had one been available, were a seldom-used luxury in those days. After a while, the single unfluctuating note of the all-clear blasted the now peaceful air and children who had not forsaken us for the quiet serenity of the Welsh valleys darted out of doorways searching for prized pieces of shrapnel and shellcases.

It was only a matter of time before the peace of our bomb-scarred and shell-torn town would again be shattered but, meantime, our typically British townspeople carried on with their respective lives and made plans to 'get things done while it's quiet'. At fifteen and the youngest member of the family, my parents were anxious that I move to a less hazardous place than Dover had become at that particular time

Having left school at fourteen, I worked for a kindly local couple for 5/- (25 pence) a week for a year, then to better myself joined the domestic staff at the nearby Isolation Hospital. The matron was a martinet of the first order and my first task of the day was to scrub the tiled floor outside her office. I had been told by the other girls that when matron came downstairs in the morning, I must stand to attention by my bucket.

I assumed they were pulling my leg, having heard from various sources of the glass hammer and buckets of steam tricks pulled on unsuspecting newcomers to a job and, on my first morning, was dutifully scrubbing the black and white tiles when matron, an austere Florence Nightingale figure in dark gown and starched white cap appeared on the stairs. I looked up, smiled a nervous 'Good morning, matron,' and continued with my task .

'Good morning, Violet. In future please remember to stop whatever you are doing and stand up when I come down in the morning.' So saying, she swept into her office, leaving me flushed with embarrassment, inwardly praying that she would quickly vacate that room before I went in to clean it, or I was certain that I would break something, or otherwise disgrace myself.

There were half-believed hints from the porters and other girls that soon it would be my turn to clean the tiny building which served as the hospital mortuary, when, if it was occupied, I would be required to move the occupant aside in order to clean the marble slab. Each new day dawned with the mounting fear that this would be the one when I would be called upon to perform this terrifying task. After all, they weren't kidding about matron, were they?

There was at that time a severe outbreak of German measles and, in an attempt to prevent it spreading throughout the various barracks in our garrison town, cases were rushed immediately to hospital. Every bed was occupied and I, a diminutive five foot nothing, almost lost my footing trying to master the heavy swing-handled 'dummies' with which we polished the wards, first spreading the orange antiseptic Ronuk on to a piece of blanket and placing under the dummy, then, with a clean piece, swung the dummy to produce a brilliant shine; I was not helped by the cheers of encouragement from the convalescing patients.

I remember in particular an ATS girl who was kept in strict isolation in the cubicled Ward 7, where, as a six year old, I had spent an uncomfortable three weeks suffering from scarlet fever. Rumour had it that she was in a very bad way having contracted spotted fever and meningitis. Working quietly with my mop wrung out in strong disinfectant, nervously keeping my distance, I jumped when she asked if I would be going out that day. She was probably no more than twenty, with dark eyes and short brown hair contrasting with her thin pale face. We usually had two or three hours off in the afternoon, going in again to serve the patients tea and, later, supper, so I asked if I could get anything for her. She asked me to hand her the purse which was on her locker; she extracted a sixpence, with great difficulty, being unable to move her head, or sit up. 'Would you get me some writing paper and envelopes, please?' she said, and I replied that I would bring them in at tea-time.

Having mentioned the matter during our dinner break, I was surprised when an irate ward sister waylaid me. She stormed that I ought to know better and insisted that I should hand the money to her. I felt that I had let the poor patient down badly but there was nothing I could do about it, sister's word being law. I never saw the poor girl again and when I heard that she had died, I decided that hospital life was not for me.

After a quiet start to the war, the phoney war as it was known, when sirens sounded but all turned out to be false alarms, things began to warm up; we would be roused from our beds and scurry down to our Anderson shelter, which my parents had furnished with benches, cushions and an old convertible bed-chair. A candlestick, candles and matches were kept in readiness but, although my mother and I, with Rex, our faithful old dog, would sleep fitfully at times, my father, much to my mother's concern, refused to leave the house, saying that he'd had enough of sleeping in trenches in the last war. The night skies displayed a dazzling, frightening display of exploding ack-ack shells and streamers of red tracer bullets. The air was heavy with the drone of aircraft which provoked speculation as to whether they were 'ours' or 'theirs' and peaceful nights were few and far between.

Through an agency, my mother arranged for me to take a job in Carshalton, Surrey, which, being in the suburbs, would, she hoped, be less liable to attack. Unfortunately, no sooner had I commenced work, which entailed looking after two children, working in the house, and occasionally serving in the baker's shop, than the raids on London began. My nights were again spent in an Anderson, larger, this time, but with the children, two adults and the occasional addition of another girl of about my age, when it was not considered safe for her to travel back to her home in Wallington. Sleeping literally like sardines, it was a case of when one turns, we all turn.

Listening to the sound of incendiary bombs, pattering down like hailstones and the booming of the mobile guns, I decided that if I was going to be bombed, I would prefer it to be on my own territory. Having notified my parents of my impending return, I gave my employers a week's notice.

When France capitulated, and the channel ports were occupied by the enemy, cross-channel shelling was inflicted on the already over-burdened populace of my home town. The monster shells landed without warning and, only after one or more had exploded, could the shell warning (one siren followed by another) be sounded. One hour after the last shell had landed the all-clear would sound, but as it was often followed by further bombardment, the effect on our nerves was considerable. A visit to the cinema, when we had expected to see the film *For Whom the Bell Tolls* resulted in an uncomfortable night cooped up in the cinema basement. As dawn broke, the owner of a cafe opposite, who was among the patrons, took advantage of a quiet period to supply us all with a welcome cup of tea and bread and butter. After thirteen hours fasting, the simple snack seemed like a feast. I listened, not daring to sleep, while tales were bandied about by my fellow prisoners of the effect of blast and of how a lady of their acquaintance, sitting between her daughter and grand-daughter, vanished without trace, while the others were comparatively unharmed.

Shortly before my return to Dover, the powers-that-be at the local paper mill had considered it expedient to split up their work force and integrate them with other branches of the firm in less vulnerable areas, so my sister's husband was offered the chance to work in a mill in Hampshire which specialised in making the paper for banknotes. Part of the Dover mill had already been damaged by a shot-down Spitfire which we watched as it came down hoping to see the pilot bale out; at one point it seemed that it was falling in our direction so we hurried to our Anderson shelter but next day we heard that it had crashed on the mill.

He was told that accommodation would be provided, so he and my sister regretfully left their own cosy home, wondering if they would ever see it again, their lives having already been disrupted by the evacuation, after much heart-searching, of their five year old daughter to Wales. My mother, always with my interests at heart, bless her, wrote to ask them to find a suitable job for me and so it was that I was leaving home to work in an evacuation camp for schoolboys from Southampton.

We reached the station without further mishap. My mother bought my ticket and obtained a platform ticket from the machine, which stood alongside the Nestlé's machines, empty now, but where a slim bar of chocolate could have been bought for the price of two pennies not too long ago. The platforms were crowded with servicemen, kitbags and all the paraphernalia of a busy station in wartime, civilians being very much in the minority. A perspiring soldier, indicating a poster on the wall, turned to his companion and groaned, 'Is our journey *really* necessary?'

The few civilian women present were either waiting to meet a husband or sweetheart, or standing with a serviceman, willing the train to be late, and so delay the inevitable parting. Young men out of uniform, engaged perhaps, in work of 'national importance', were sending wives with young families off to stay with relatives in less vulnerable areas, 'for the duration'.

My mother fussed over me, saying that she wished she could see me safely through London, to be sure to get a cup of tea before getting the west-bound train, and to write as soon as I reached my destination. I

15

laughed and told her not to worry, but I shared her unease at parting in such uncertain times.

The train arrived and drew to a halt with a noisy hiss of escaping steam. I thought of happier days when, armed with bucket and spade, I had jumped back in alarm at the approach of the noisy iron monster. I managed to find a seat, my luggage was hoisted on to the rack by an obliging young airman, I exchanged final goodbyes with my mother and, with mixed feelings of regret and anticipation, saw the familiar station recede into the distance before the train was swallowed up in the tunnel under the chalk downs.

The journey was uneventful and I was glad to leave the crowded carriage at Waterloo. After buying a cup of tea from a station trolley, which tasted as if it had been made with water from the engine, I successfully crossed to the west-bound train; this was much less crowded and I sat back and enjoyed the sandwiches that my mother had prepared for me.

The bomb-scarred buildings of London and neat houses of the suburbs gave way to green fields where sheep and cows grazed contentedly, and the golden stubble of recently harvested corn, peaceful land, unmarked by the bombers which flew over in search of their targets in more densely populated areas. My mind drifted back over the events of the past two troubled years. The crisis of 1938 when war had appeared imminent, and when I, in my last full year at school, had been given a form asking my parents' consent to my being evacuated to a safe area in the event of war. How well I remembered the hollow sinking feeling I experienced, and how I insisted that I did not want to be evacuated. 'If you are going to be bombed, I'd rather be bombed too.'

The short-lived relief when the well meaning but misguided Neville Chamberlain waved in the air the worthless piece of paper proclaiming 'Peace in our time'. The issue of Anderson and (later) Morrison shelters, the construction of public shelters and the forming of Civil Defence units; air raid wardens, street wardens, the Auxiliary Fire Service, and the stirrup pumps issued to every tenth house to be used to extinguish incendiary bombs.

The notices which appeared all over town urging residents to collect their gas-masks and to wear them for a short period each day in order to get used to them – and the mild amusement when we discovered the rude noises they emitted when air was expelled from the sides. There were gas-masks designed to protect babies which, thank God, were never needed.

Articles in newspapers urged householders to tape windows to prevent injury from flying glass and to prepare emergency kits of food, water and first aid equipment.

Streets and gardens were torn apart to house shelters and the caves under the cliffs were opened as shelters, complete with tiered bunks. All these events led to that fateful Sunday morning, 3rd September 1939 when, at eleven o'clock, the Prime Minister broadcast to the nation that we were at war with Germany. Almost immediately sirens wailed over the town which previously had echoed only to the sound of church bells, soon to be silenced and sounded only in the unthinkable event of invasion.

Although I didn't as a general rule, work on Sundays, I had been asked by my first employers if I would go in on Sunday as they were having friends in for a meal. Immediately the Prime Minister's speech ended, I picked up my bag to walk the mile or so to work, my mother hastily put on her coat and said, 'I'll walk down with you, I want to call into Partridges to get a tin of peas.' Never had I known my mother to go shopping on a Sunday, but I was glad of her company as far as the little general shop which was about half-way to my destination, especially when the chilling sound of the sirens filled the air.

At the outbreak of war, schools, in common with cinemas, theatres and other places where large numbers of people would gather, closed for an indefinite period.

Parents, in areas considered vulnerable to attack, faced the heartrending choice of allowing their children to be transported to 'places of safety' or keeping them at home. An unenviable task. If the parents perished, how would their orphaned children fare? If they let them stay, and their little ones were injured or worse, they would carry the guilt for the rest of their lives. Many parents did consent to relinquish their hold on their young ones and, from all the risk areas, children were sent away with their small case containing clothes and a favourite toy, the square box containing their gas-mask hanging from each small shoulder.

The depression years of the thirties did not allow many luxuries. The kids brought up in those days were content with their lot, little though it may have been but it might have included a whip and top, marbles, meccano or a favourite book, doll or teddy bear. They knew it was no use crying for the moon, for the moon was not theirs to be had. And so the pathetic queues for transport formed, with the mothers trying to save their own tears until they returned to their strangely quiet homes, telling the children that they were going for a nice holiday in the country, how lucky they were, and how they wished they were going too. Many of the children were tearful, bewildered and not altogether sure that they approved of this unexpected holiday. Some, mature beyond their years, regarded the prospect of a new way of life away from the smoky cities as something to be tried for a while, anyway, a holiday from which they could return if they found it not to their liking. Their final destination was something in the nature of pot luck. Many suffered the indignity of being left until last as would-be foster parents chose first the most personable among them.

Some found themselves in homes little different from the ones they had left behind and, on arriving, tired, hungry and dishevelled, were welcomed with open arms. Others were placed in middle and upper class residences where they were kindly treated but never really felt that they belonged. Many formed friendships which have endured to this day, but wherever they found themselves, however kind and well-meaning their foster parents, they could not take the place of the parents they had left behind. The song *Goodnight children everywhere, your daddy thinks of you tonight*, drifting all too frequently from the wireless in many a temporary home, reduced the sensitive youngsters to tears. So devastating was the effect, particularly on those whose fathers were on active service, that the song, recalling cosy evenings at home, and *Children's Hour* on the wireless was banned by the BBC.

Children from London's East End, many of whom had never seen a cow, thrived in the country air and most, resilient as kids are, stayed for the duration, occasionally going home for short holidays, rummaging among the debris for souvenirs to be borne proudly back for inspection by the children who were native to the safe areas.

Many of the foster parents invited the parents of their new charges to spend a few days with them if space permitted. These invitations were gratefully accepted, the money for the train fare being scraped together somehow, and the parents returned home relieved in some small way that they could now conjure up a mental picture of their young ones in their new surroundings.

My thoughts jerked back to the present and I became aware of boards by the side of the track flashing by stating 'You are now entering the Strong country' and, later, 'You are now IN the Strong country'. After all my protestations against being evacuated as a schoolgirl, here I was, virtually an evacuee myself, except that I would be working for a living.

I was feeling hot and a little sleepy, but kept my eyes and ears open, for in wartime Britain place names were obliterated in anticipation of the expected invasion and, at last, at a tiny village station set in the heart of the country, I heard a voice with an unfamiliar rounded accent call out the name of my destination, Overton. I hauled my cases down from the rack, and was relieved to see my sister, Lily, waiting on the otherwise deserted platform. Having exchanged family news, she took one of my cases and said she would show me the bed-sitting-room which was now her temporary home, so that I would know where to go when I had time off to visit them.

We walked down the dry, dusty path from the station, past the watercress beds, the tiny village church and down the aptly named Bridge Street to the main road through the village, where, passing the Red Lion on the corner, we reached the house owned by an elderly couple, a retired postman and his wife, in which my sister and her husband Charlie had a ground floor room and the use of the kitchen. My sister had already set the table and, while making a pot of tea in the kitchen, introduced me to her landlady, Mrs Brown, a pleasant woman with brown eyes and greyish white hair swept into a bun. We went back into the room and my sister placed the teapot on the table which was near the window.

A brass-knobbed iron bed occupied a third of the space and an armchair stood on either side of the fireplace, above which protruded an as yet unlit gaslamp. We giggled softly at the sight of the pheasant feathers which sprouted from vases and behind pictures. Lily said she had taken them down and put them in a drawer, holding the dust as they did, but had to display them again, as her landlady seemed upset at their absence.

After tea, my sister produced a writing pad and envelopes and we each wrote a brief note to our parents informing them of my safe arrival. 'If you are ready,' she said, 'I'll show you where the post office is and we'll get this off right away.' Telegrams were not sent lightly, harbingers of bad news that they had become, but, moistening the royal blue 2d stamp, we were confident that our letter would reach its destination – barring a direct hit from Jerry, of course. Picking up the cases and retracing our steps into Bridge Street, I saw at the far end an old house, partly screened by trees, which I had not noticed before. I learned later, according to one of the girls at the camp, that on one of the ceilings was a blood stain, which, no matter how often it was washed or painted over, always re-appeared. I was to hear many of these stories. We turned left up a gently sloping lane, with hedges of varying height on either side, broken by the occasional barred gate through which could be seen fields and haystacks. The flat landscape seemed strange after the green hills spiked with guns which, against the skyline, looked like giant school compasses which surrounded my home town. The blue sky, as evening approached, had given way to subtle shades of apricot and gold.

'I didn't mention it before,' said my sister, 'but a couple of weeks ago some bombs were dropped on a sewage farm just up the road. It's usually quiet, though, and I think you'll like working at the camp. Mr and Mrs Davies seem very nice people.'

'Jerry must have heard that I was coming,' I joked. 'It was quiet at Carshalton until I went there.' Rumour had it that the pilot responsible for the near miss on the camp had been shot down and was reduced to tears to learn that his target was a children's camp and not the military depot he had imagined it to be.

A few minutes later we reached the gates of Lords Field camp. A broad asphalt drive stretched before us, with blue and white painted wooden buildings on either side, slightly raised from the ground under which could be seen yellowed grass starved of sunlight, in contrast to the green well-kept verges. Each bungalow had two flights of steps leading to two doors at the front and a door at each end.

The first bungalow, I learned, was occupied by the headmaster, Mr Collins, and his wife; concrete paths laid over the turf led on to the next which was occupied by Mr and Mrs Davies. Another path led to the bungalow, which, it turned out, was to be my home for the next three years. It was occupied by never less than four, and sometimes as many as ten girls. The next bungalow housed the male staff. On our left was the matron's home and sick bay, and behind were several dormitories, classrooms and an assembly hall.

Ahead, at the end of the drive, I could see several green-overalled girls through the windows of another large building. We stopped, however, at the second bungalow, my sister rang the bell, and I stood back feeling a little apprehensive.

I need not have worried, the manager and his wife were charming; they invited us into their cosily carpeted sitting room, furnished with brown leather, velvet cushioned armchairs. On a shelf above the electric fire, an array of beautifully ornamental jugs caught my eye. These, I learned, were antique Welsh jugs, and it was to be one of my duties to dust them, as I was to be appointed manager's maid, combined with the other duties of table laying, washing up and all the other tasks which made for the smooth running of the camp.

We spent a very pleasant hour with my new employers, while Mrs Davies made tea and enquired about life in Hellfire Corner, commiserating with my sister at having to leave her home. I was grateful to Lily for having gone to the trouble of visiting the camp and securing the job for me, relieving the anxiety my parents had felt when the raids had become increasingly severe. Mr Davies had sent the money for my train fare; for that, too, I was thankful, as there was little money to spare for anything other than necessities. He, also, did everything possible to put me at ease, joking in his bluff, open way, teasing his plump little wife, and enquiring after my family; it was difficult to get the right type of girl, he said, in his pleasant Welsh voice, but he was extremely satisfied with his present staff and he was sure that I would be happy working with them. 'After all, fair play, I am not as daunting as Hitler, am I?'

2: Mrs Davies with Shaun

21

He ventured information as to the amenities of the village, where, he said, there were many ladies who helped them out temporarily at very short notice; indeed, he said, one of our most reliable girls lives in the village, as did some of the male staff.

A childless couple, having been married late in life, they lavished their affections on Shaun, a beautiful white and tortoise-shell Persian cat which had travelled to Hampshire with them. I soon discovered that they had the interests of their entire staff at heart and no legitimate grievance went unheeded; their genuine concern won the loyalty of us all.

As we talked, I glanced through the prettily curtained windows; groups of boys, clad mostly in grey pullovers and knee-length grey trousers were streaming down the drive, making the most of the last hour of daylight before the long autumn evening imprisoned them in their dormitories. Some appeared to be no more than seven or eight years of age, but all seemed to be in good spirits; some, arms outstretched, zoomed along imitating aeroplanes, while others emitted staccato noises as if to shoot down the planes with imaginary guns. Banished from home though they were, it would take more than Hitler to quell their natural high spirits. Our preliminary chat concluded, Mrs Davies escorted me, accompanied by my sister, into the staff bungalow.

'Put your cases down by yer,' she said in her lilting Welsh accent, indicating a bed by the end window. There were six beds at that time, each with a bedside locker and an under-bed locker which comfortably housed full length coats and dresses laid flat and utilised space to the best advantage. Above each green-quilted bed were railings with green curtains, which could be swished round for privacy, and thick green curtains, lined with blackout material, were drawn back from the windows. At the far end, an open door revealed a sitting room with table, chairs and a wireless, with an extension speaker in the sleeping quarters. The bungalow was centrally heated; a neat pile of clothes and an electric iron stood on a stand on the table and various items of clothing festooned the radiators. My sister, having seen me safely settled in, took her leave, and Mrs Davies led me across to the scullery introducing me to the girls who were drying stacks of strong white cups and plates which had been passed through an enormous dishwasher. Next to the scullery was the kitchen, efficiently run by two well-qualified chefs and kitchen porters.

To familiarise myself as to where things were kept, I followed the girls who were carrying stacks of plates and trays of cups through a door, where a large, steel-topped hot-plate separated the kitchen area from the dining hall. About forty tables, each capable of seating eight boys were spaced at regular intervals; at each end of the hall were long tables, which seated domestic staff at one end and teaching staff at the other. Through a closed door at the teachers' end was the masters' common room, fairly comfortably furnished and usually littered with newspapers and general paper-work. It doubled as an observation room, with large windows on three sides from which one could see almost the entire camp.

At the opposite end were the stores and a shop run by Mrs Davies, where we could buy shampoos and cosmetics, when available. Through the large windows of the dining hall, I was surprised to see sheep grazing; these were cared for by the boys, who also kept rabbits and bees and tended gardens at the rear of the dormitories. Having tidied the dining hall, the girls trooped into the kitchen to collect their own supper. Staff and masters had their meals at the same time, although the masters had devised a relay system in order to supervise the boys. The girl whose turn it was to wait at their table was given her meal early. The food, considering wartime shortages, was very good, usually soup, a main course and sweet or cheese and biscuits were served at dinner and supper, often at the expense of the young evacuees, who were served much plainer fare.

I collected my soup and joined the rest of the staff at the table; someone switched on the wireless and the announcer on the BBC Home Service read, using the under-statement considered necessary to boost the morale, and confuse the enemy, 'In a south-eastern coastal town two barrage balloons had been shot down that morning by a single enemy aircraft.' There was no doubt in my mind that it referred to the incident I had witnessed on my way to the station that morning. Names of towns were seldom mentioned; 'Somewhere in England' became a national catch-phrase.

Having finished the meal, I helped the other girls dry the dishes. Someone found me some green overalls and caps with NCC (for National Camps Corporation) embroidered on the pockets and brim. We strolled over to the bungalow and, having pulled the blackout curtains settled down for a chat before preparing for bed. There were three other girls in the bungalow at that time. Margaret, a local girl, plumply pretty, fair and motherly, who was later to regale us with stories of strange local legends; Jenny, a Welsh girl, tall, dark and sturdily built; and cockney Florrie from London, plump and fortyish. Two other girls who had accompanied Mr and Mrs Davies (a former mayor and mayoress of Merthyr Tydfil), from Wales, shared a room in another part of the camp. Most had been at the camp since its inception and, while others came and went, they, along with four others and myself, became firmly established. The hours were long perhaps, by today's standards; we went on duty at 7 am, and worked through until our supper at about 9 pm, with two or three hours break for resting, reading, or personal chores during the afternoon. Our day commenced with a cup of tea in the kitchen, after which we set the tables for the boys' breakfast, which was usually porridge (irreverently referred to as 'skilley' by the boys) or corn flakes, followed by bacon or French toast, (bread dipped in beaten egg and fried golden brown), bangers, or rather solidified fried eggs, which had, of necessity, been prepared well in advance. Dried egg powder, issued by the Ministry of Food, made quite palatable scrambled egg, once one had become accustomed to the somewhat leathery texture, although there were those who argued that it was debatable if it had ever seen the inside of a shell.

While preparations were being made for breakfast, the boys, having been roused by the morning bell, were busily engaged in showering and bed-making, before parading, army fashion, in all but the most inclement weather, for breakfast at 8.30. Discipline was very strict and late-comers were punished by the 'dreaded stick'. One such caning was usually sufficient to ensure that the young offender was more punctual on future parades.

A clumping of feet on the wooden verandah outside the dining hall heralded the orderly arrival of the boys, who stood smartly by their tables until all were present. Clad in short trousers, the cheeky, the studious, the obviously homesick, they displayed a well-scrubbed cheerfulness but one suspected that under the bright facade lurked many a bewildered, lonely little boy, a secret to be shared only with the often damp pillow which did nothing to soften the hardness of his double-decker bed.

I cannot say with any certainty that grace was said before the meal, but in all probability, in keeping with the times when scripture was as much a lesson as any other in the curriculum and not the optional extra which it has become today, a short prayer was offered. Table by table, the boys filed by the hotplate to collect their ration, all expressing a polite 'Thank you, miss,' the bolder among them sometimes uttering an additional disparaging remark as to the composition of the offered meal. 'Cor, skilley again,' 'What's this, rat stew?' always with a wary eye on chef.

Once seated, the meal was eaten with only a quiet murmur of conversation, broken by the occasional stentorian boom of a surname, as one of the youngsters committed some minor offence. Any food remaining after the first serving was given as second helpings, the tables being taken in strict rotation, while at least four girls walked round pouring tea from large green and cream enamel pots. The meal completed, the boys awaited the order to stack the fast-emptied dishes on to the hotplate, where they were collected by the girls and passed through the scalding water in the dishwasher, all leavings being first deposited in the large pig-bin housed under the scrubbed wooden table. Thus fortified, the boys were marshalled out to the classrooms to commence the day's lessons.

Having restored the scullery to a state of order, we enjoyed a reasonably leisurely breakfast, then carried out our respective duties before returning to serve the boys' dinner, a fairly substantial meal, with pudding to follow. One of the chefs would officiate and with a flourish ladle out the stew, or whatever constituted the main meal, while the senior girls dished out the vegetables and gravy. A favourite sweet was carrot flan piped with mock cream. Made with the chef's expertise, it tasted every bit as delicious as a more conventional one made of fruit. Tinned fruit was, of course, virtually unobtainable. Tea was a simple meal of bread and jam, or golden syrup, and perhaps cake. In summer, lemonade was sometimes substituted for the usual tea. Supper consisted of bread and milk, bread and butter and cocoa, or a slice of bread covered with gravy. By the time we had cleared up and eaten our more substantial supper, it was well after nine o'clock and, after reading, or listening to the wireless, it was lights out, blackouts drawn back, and off to bed.

It is significant of the change in standards of behaviour that the bungalows were left unlocked and unattended for most of the day, and only locked at night – and then only to give us a sense of security, for we were, after all, in a remote country area. In all the time I was at Lords Field, nothing to the best of my knowledge was stolen, and there was no vandalism, apart from that of one boy whose repeated unsuccessful efforts to light a bonfire under the assembly hall became a source of some amusement, although his efforts did not go unpunished.

Boys being boys, there were, of course, minor scraps and disagreements but violence as we know it today was not even contemplated. Could it be that with so much destruction all around, and with our very existence threatened, the only thought uppermost in the minds of us all was to rebuild, repair and live in peace?

The amount of pocket money received by the boys probably varied according to the financial status of the parents but, until sweet rationing was introduced, there were no sweets available; nor were bananas or oranges to be had, the convoys facing the ever constant threat of the U-boats had space only for the most essential food-stuffs. Many shops, however, did offer for sale carrots, advertised as a healthy alternative to sweets (and even as an aid to seeing in the black-out), for a halfpenny each. To earn extra pocket money, boys helped local farmers by fruit and potato picking.

For my part, I was paid 12/6, (62.5 pence), with food and board provided. A local shop, Howard's, provided a fairly comprehensive library service and, for a reasonable charge of 2d, we borrowed books to read in our rather limited free time, usually on wet afternoons and Sundays, when, as some of the boys went home for the weekend, only the essential jobs were undertaken.

On my one half-day off, I visited my sister, or went to the old cinema at Whitchurch, four miles from the village, or alternatively further afield to Basingstoke or Andover, to shop, have tea, and invariably end up at 'the pictures'. Everywhere, it seemed, were posters urging one to 'Make do and mend', 'Be like dad, keep mum', 'Dig for victory', and reminders that 'Careless talk costs lives', and 'Walls have ears', under which some wag was certain to have added 'Ice cream'. The red painted snack bar by the bus depot at Andover, where one could buy hot drinks and sandwiches was very popular with passengers awaiting their particular bus.

The juke box blared out popular Glen Miller songs, *Jersey Bounce* and *Take the A-train*. The smartly uniformed Yanks, waiting for transport to Salisbury, Odiham and the various airfields which it seemed they had entirely taken over, would, on five minutes' acquaintance, beg every available girl, 'Marry me, and I'll take you back to the States.'

Although the frequent nightly excursions of one short-stay glamour girl extracted from an older member of staff that 'She's no better than she should be,' we were, I believe, a very moral lot and at least two of our charming allies discovered that not all British girls could be bought for the price of a pair of nylons, and even insisted on 'going Dutch'.

Italian prisoners of war from a nearby camp walked round quite freely in their distinctive brown uniform with large orange patches. They helped out on the farms and, to while away the hours, made wooden toys which were sold quite cheaply locally. Wooden dogs on wheels, which nodded their heads when pulled along by the attached string, ducks which flapped their wings and chickens which, by a deceptively simple arrangement of strings connected to a piece of carved wood no bigger than a walnut, appeared to peck at the poker-burned holes representing grain on the base resembling a table-tennis bat, through which the strings were threaded.

Returning to the camp on summer evenings, the haystacks behind the hedges could be heard literally rustling and rats would scamper across the road no more than a few yards ahead of us. We got used to them, but approached the kitchen warily, knowing that they went foraging round the swill-bins. The chefs would always leave supper for us on our half-days off, shepherds pie, sardines on toast, or spam and salad, which we enjoyed at our leisure. On returning, we invariably called in at our bungalow first, seeking the company of the other girls, just in case there were any rats near the kitchen.

Two old men of near retiring age did odd jobs and kept the swill-bins and outhouses scrupulously clean; they spoke in a soft local burr, and treated us with almost old-world courtesy. The same, alas, could not be said for some of the younger male staff, who took a delight in throwing dead rats as we were walking near the boiler room or incinerator, calculated to hit the wall just in front of us and, on more than one occasion, we were horrified to find a dead rat hidden under the clean tea towels that we had hung to dry overnight on the dishwasher racks, placed there as a macabre joke. When I celebrated my sixteenth birthday, the manager and his wife complimented me on my work, and said that they were increasing my wages to 16/- (80 pence), but that I was not to mention it to the other girls. I suspected that they treated us all in the same way, but it had the effect of making one feel appreciated.

As time went by, I copied from the example of one of the girls, and for a 2/- (10 pence) deposit, hired from the post office a money box in the shape of a book. It was about the size of an average bible, metal, of course, but fashioned to resemble green leather with gilt-edged pages. There were slots for coins and a small round hole to take rolled up 10/- or £1 notes. Did anyone earn enough to use these holes, I thought as I carefully posted in every spare penny, sixpence and shilling? The key was kept by the post-mistress, a rather stern lady, with pepper and salt coloured hair and the amount taken from the box recorded in a savings book. In my anxiety to see the written balance grow, I presented my book at the Post Office every fortnight or so, and the post-mistress, tired of entering my three and elevens, and five and twopence half-pennies, sternly requested that I wait until I had saved at least ten shillings before having the box emptied. Suitably admonished, I kept a written record of my own after that and further visits, even to buy postage stamps for my letters home, were made with some trepidation.

The demon-like 'Squander bug' leered down at us from every hoarding with captions entreating, 'Save, don't let the squander bug gobble your money'; and save we endeavoured to do, in spite of wages that were meagre, but adequate for our simple needs. For the non-smoking, non-drinking members of society there was little to purchase, anyway. Sweets, before rationing, were snapped up as soon as they appeared – there was always some eagle-eyed passer-by to divulge the news that a delivery had been made. The hard-pressed shopkeeper, faced with the difficult task of devising his own system of rationing, kept them 'under the counter', and served only his most valued customers, so limited were the supplies which trickled into his sadly depleted store room.

Familiar brand names disappeared from many goods, some never to return. My first lipstick, a fiery red refill in a scrap of cellophane, stung my lips; heaven and the manufacturer alone knew what unmentionable ingredients went into that greasy crayon which had a sting equal to that of a tropical insect. Thanks to Mrs Davies, we were able to purchase powders and creams to boost our morale, and those who favoured eye make-up concocted a mixture of boot polish and vaseline which made a passable mascara. Fullers earth mixed with water made face-packs, and we lay on our beds, green-faced and grotesque, threatening death to anyone who caused us to laugh and crack the hard chalky death masks which would have done justice to the make-up department of a horror movie.

We joked light-heartedly, though news of casualties at home and abroad were broadcast daily. One of the girls became increasingly worried at the lack of news from her 'young man' who was serving overseas. My mother wrote that she had not heard from my eldest brother for several weeks. We used the stock phrase, 'there is probably a holdup in the post', which was of very little comfort.

Chapter Two

MASS BREAKOUT

ONE OF THE HIGHLIGHTS OF THE BOYS' YEAR, except for the Sundays when a special tea was laid on for the parents and relatives who arrived by the coachload, was the school concert, when they performed various sketches and songs with enthusiasm and a professionalism that were a credit to the masters who coached them, .

The theme song, sung to the tune of: *Darling Clementine*, began:

> On a hill above a valley
>   Stands a camp, a lovely camp,
> Where Southampton boys are sheltered
>   From the cold and from the damp.

The opening bars would be greeted with howls of derision, laughingly condoned by the teaching staff, discipline being temporarily relaxed. The domestic staff were always invited to these shows and the boyish voices, coupled with the deep resonant tones of the masters, echoed round the hall:-

> Oh! the classrooms, Oh! the dining hall,
>   Oh! the dormitories five,
> Where the masters and the matron
>   Strive to keep us all alive.

The song embraced practically every aspect of the camp, from kitchen to ablutions. One year, a party of mummers, resplendent in flowing medieval dress, added their traditional silent, miming talents to the Christmas show.

On visiting days, we set the tables with a special tea, which included

29

fruit cake, for the eagerly awaited visitors, and we watched from the scullery windows as the blue and cream Summerbees coaches drew to a standstill.

The expressions of absolute joy on the faces of those boys who were lucky enough to have a much loved mother, grandparent or younger brother or sister alight from one of the coaches was a joy to behold, while our hearts went out to those not so fortunate, who wandered around aimlessly, trying to appear nonchalant. Fathers, apart from the dockers and those turning out the legendary Spitfires, whose work was of national importance and were consequently exempt from call-up, were mostly conspicuous by their absence, many being in the services, leaving a wife to carry on as bravely as she could and having no alternative but to allow sons, for their own safety, to be torn from a loving home into the rough and tumble of an all male society, completely bewildered that this war, which was not of their making, should snatch them from the more relaxed rules of parental guidance, to the stern atmosphere of perpetual school discipline, when all they wanted, like most boys, was to shrug off the shackles of school at the end of the day for the quiet security of tea at home with mum and dad and a comic by the fire.

The happy reunions passed all too quickly and the visitors were escorted manfully back to the waiting coaches. Later, at supper, those faces which had registered such joy a short time before, were, along with those boys who had not received a visitor, pale and trying hard not to show the desolation that was in the hearts of the once again deserted evacuees.

The boys were treated well, although very sternly disciplined, but homesickness, especially when Southampton had been subjected to air raids, led inevitably to absenteeism, when boys would attempt, with varying degrees of success, to follow the railway lines back to their home town, some thirty miles away. They were severely punished, when, as was inevitable, they were brought back to the camp; railway lines, although not electrified at that time, were not the safest of places on which to travel on foot. We protested when they were caned in the dining hall in our presence, knowing a little of the homesickness which we all experienced at times.

One day there was great consternation in the camp when the boys staged a mass breakout, which became the topic of conversation for many a long day and night, as they swapped stories of their adventures in the darkened dormitories. Not all the boys were involved, but enough were missing to cause a great deal of activity in the camp. Some, we heard later, had gone well prepared with sandwiches (made with bread bought in the village and spread with the contents of jars brought by the visitors), wellingtons and warm clothes. The weather had not left the ground in an ideal condition for the young escapees; thin shoes and knee length socks soon became uncomfortably wet for those who decided to join their schoolfellows on a spur of the moment basis in the mass exit from what must at times seemed like a prison; were they not being held against their will and punished when they put into action their very real desires to visit home and family?

What had started as a mere trickle became a grey and navy blanket as, lemming like, they streamed down the field and through the fence to freedom. The police, of course, were informed and within a day or two all the boys were brought back, some having reached their goal, Southampton; others, cold, tired and hungry, gave up miles from home. What had caused this mass exodus no one knew, unless they had perhaps seen a film of a prison escape, but it was probably a mixture of homesickness, a taste for adventure and rebellion against the strict discipline, but they returned by car, van and on foot from the station.

Some, at least, were obviously thankful to be back to the warmth and safety of the camp after the long, dark night when planes and gunfire had

3: The Author with the dormitories
in the background

made their ominous contribution to the no less frightening sounds of rustling bushes and eerie howling of the wind, even though the threat of the inevitable canings loomed like a spectre in each tired young mind. The adventure was over, the minds of those who had managed to reach home were set at rest and it was back to the daily routine.

The staff, of course, were in sympathy with the young rebels, but were nevertheless thankful to see them all safely back in the fold.

One evening, at supper, the drone of bomb-laden aircraft could be heard. 'Doan like the sound o' they,' said Harry, one of the locally-born male staff.

'Goin' to S'thampton, I'll bet,' volunteered another.

'They might be ours,' said one of the girls, which, when the planes had passed over without incident, provoked a discussion as to how one could distinguish an enemy plane from one of ours.

'Well,' said young Harry, with a wink, (the significance of which escaped us at the time), 'if they've got turned up tails, then's the time to run.'

I must admit that in spite of witnessing any number of dog-fights in my home town, the only planes which I could identify with any degree of accuracy were Spitfires, Lysanders and the Dakotas from the nearby US Air Force bases at Sutton Scotney and Barton Stacey.

The next afternoon I accompanied two of the girls to the library in the village; on the way down we heard the drone of approaching aircraft. Scanning the sky and with the previous evening's conversation fresh in our minds, we saw flying towards us at a fairly low altitude three planes – and each had a turned up tail!

With one accord, we threw ourselves into the by no means dry ditch by the hedge. The planes flew unconcernedly on, their occupants totally unaware of the havoc which they had unwittingly created in their own green and pleasant land. Realisation suddenly dawned, didn't *all* planes have turned up tails? We fell about laughing, only sobering when we examined the mudstains on our coats.

'Wait until I see that so-and-so,' said one of my less than immaculate companions, 'I'll *do* him.' This, with a little help from her friends she proceeded to do as soon as the opportunity arose, tickling him until his hoarse shouts for mercy brought workmates to his rescue. Some time later, my brother, who was deaf since a bombing raid when he was a small baby in the first world war and was therefore exempt from military service, filled a vacancy on the male staff; he was a very diligent and conscientious worker and played his part in the general maintenance of the camp. As more girls joined the staff, Mr Davies decided that we could each have a full day off, which meant that for the first time we could take turns to sleep late on one morning in the week but we discovered that for some obscure psychological reason, the long-awaited 'lie-ins' did not materialise as, when we could have slept late, we were wide awake and, on our duty days, we were reluctant to leave our beds.

The local girls, of course, were able to go home after duty on the evening prior to their day off. We each had a jam jar, which was refilled with our six ounce sugar ration each week, and a dish for our 'national' butter and margarine, part of the ration being withheld for cooking purposes and, because of rationing, I didn't consider it fair to spend the entire day with my sister, who already cheerfully provided me with tea on some of my half days off and always rustled up a snack when I dropped in for an hour on my off duty breaks. So, on mornings off I enjoyed the luxury of breakfast in bed, the meal being brought over on a tray by one of the girls. I caught up with letter writing, sewing, etc., and made my way to Andover or Basingstoke, where, for 1s/6d, a favourite cafe provided Welsh rarebit and tea or feeling wickedly extravagant as I parted with my half-crown (12.5p), indulged in a knickerbocker glory, a mouth-watering concoction of real fruit, jelly and ice cream before the inevitable visit to the pictures. Remote as we were from air raids, any feelings of complacency were soon dispelled at the sight of servicemen, usually airmen, from the hospital at Park Prewitt, Basingstoke, who had undergone plastic surgery on their faces, or who walked round with their arms supported on frames, often accompanied by fellow patients cheerfully hobbling on crutches.

When we had a full complement of staff, we were all delighted to hear that we were each to be allowed a free weekend in rotation, those of us who came from a distance being granted an extra day for travelling, so I was able to visit my parents every three months. I discovered, however, that before going to Dover I would have to write and obtain a permit from the chief constable, which seemed strange as I was born there, but it was all in the cause of security. Travelling at night in blacked-out trains was a nerve-racking experience; there were seldom any seats to be had and most of the journey was spent in crowded corridors with only a suitcase to sit on. Always, especially when nearing London, there was the fear of bombing, trains and railways being among the prime targets.

Already, in the draughty underground stations, the people of London had begun their nightly pilgrimage. Laden with blankets, cushions and baskets containing everything that would make the long night more bearable, sandwiches, milk for the babies and flasks of tea, that British panacea for all ills. Girls and women with Dinki curlers peeping from under neatly tied turbans contrived to make their siren-suited youngsters as comfortable as was possible in what had become almost their second home.

Joking and singing, these defiantly cheerful people kept well hidden the constant fear of what they might find when they emerged, barely refreshed, to start the new day. So it was with a heartfelt prayer of thanks that I stepped on to the familiar platform of my local station, even though the ever-present searchlight beams stabbed at the night sky. My mother and father were delighted to see me after so long an absence and there was always something special for my supper on these occasions, in spite of the worsening food situation. We were issued with emergency ration cards for long weekends, so I didn't feel that I was depriving them of their meagre rations. I was glad that I had been saving, small though the amounts were, as it enabled me to pay my fare and, as clothes rationing had been recently introduced, I asked my mother if she would accompany me to Canterbury to help me choose something new, with my as yet unused coupons.

The shoe shops were full of colourful clogs, either off ration or for less coupons than a conventional pair of shoes. With their bright red and blue straps, and thick wooden soles, they were not unlike the 'exercise sandals' that have been sold in more recent years. I purchased a skirt and short jacket for about £2/10s, £2.50) and eighteen coupons. Twenty-four coupons were issued to each person every year, with concessionary coupons for expectant mothers and children. Some people with large families, who, for one reason or another, but usually lack of money, had coupons to spare, sold them, although it was against the law, and a flourishing black market existed in coupons and other scarce commodities, but for most people the lack of coupons meant a great deal of improvisation and 'make do and mend' was the order of the day.

On one of these trips to Canterbury, we found that a recent heavy 'blitz' had practically flattened the main shopping centre, and shopkeepers were carrying on 'business as usual' in the cellars beneath the shops which were reduced to rubble. Dover, too, had more scars each time I returned home. Familiar buildings gone for ever and what was so much worse, familiar faces, among them classmates who so short a time before had gathered in the school playground. Whole families wiped out, one friend permanently blinded, her sister killed, and boys I had known all my life killed while serving their country.

One fine Sunday evening, while my mother and I were out walking, we stopped to talk to an elderly lady, her mauve floral dress making a splash of colour as she sat among the grey debris on the steps which were all that remained of her home. A widow, she gazed at the rubble where once had stood the cottage in which she had brought up her family, reliving memories of happier days. These many years later those steps remain, a grim reminder of those days when Britain stood alone. What was once a row of old but neat stone cottages has become a dumping ground for old tins and carpets, a legacy of this affluent, but discontented age, a slide where many a dusty-trousered schoolboy loiters on his way home from school. I never fail to picture that grey haired old lady, quietly and tenaciously clinging to her memories each time I pass that way.

Grim as the times undoubtedly were, people somehow managed to salvage a smile from all but the most tragic situations. One story which was circulating was of an old man who, pulling the chain in his outside toilet, marvelled at his own strength when the entire building collapsed about him. He was said to have been unhurt, his Herculean chain-pulling coinciding with a shell falling far enough away not to cause more serious damage to his property.

Winston Churchill, clad in his famous siren suit and waving his equally famous cigar, made a number of visits to Dover, inspecting the huge fourteen-inch guns which were secreted in the white cliffs (nick-named Winnie and Pooh by the troops who returned cross-fire when the mighty shells from Cap Gris Nez and Calais landed in the town), gazing out over the twenty-one mile stretch of water, which, before the invention of the aeroplane, had protected our shores from alien forces. Wendell Wilkie, a visiting American ambassador, was reported to have said, while surveying that same narrow strip of shining water, 'Keep those Goddam sons of bitches off o' these shores at all costs.'

It was chilling to know that the enemy was only twenty-one miles away, less than a third of the distance from Dover to London, and that concealed in those cliffs which could be seen from our own window on a fine day were those monstrous guns which could and did create such havoc and destruction. Frequent bombing attacks were made on shipping in the harbour, and we watched as the planes dived, screeching, to the attack. Guns from the castle and breakwater fired in defence, our own fighter planes emitting bursts of machine-gun fire, and we were ready to dive into our Anderson if the planes turned towards the town. Huge hoardings blotted out the entire seafront area and no unauthorised person (which meant almost the entire population) could catch a glimpse of the sea at close quarters; ugly tank traps and barbed wire abounded and I thought nostalgically of the days when, accompanied by Floss, my childhood pet dog, I had spent sunny, carefree days on the beach, watching the frequent arrival and departure of the giant sea-planes. Sky-writing planes spelt out 'Players, please' and 'Lamkin rugs'; then, as the white and fluffy words expanded and became indistinct, I would wade out to the wooden rafts which were anchored some yards off the shore, which seemed far away at low tide. Floss had taken her responsibility of guardianship very seriously, frantically dog-paddling so close that her claws scratched my legs.

Dotted along the seafront in those pre-war days, whose place has now been taken by cars parked bumper to bonnet, were fruit stalls where one could buy Worcester and Beauty of Bath apples and tiny sweet pink and yellow pears for 2d a pound. Pedal-powered ice-cream barrows offered for sale delicious halfpenny and penny cornets, vying with the blue and white chequered Walls 'Stop me and buy one' cycle-barrows, which sold triangular shaped sno-fruits and sno-creams and, a rare treat, this, 2d bricks. Oh! the decisions. Should we spend our precious penny on an ice cream, or approach the fruit stall, and say grandly 'Half a pound of apples (or pears), please'? Having made our choice, we returned to the beach, then, after bathing with our rubber rings, enjoyed the egg sandwiches and lemonade made with yellow lemon-flavoured sugar, packed by our mothers.

If, however, as so often happened on our unpredictable south-eastern corner of England, a chilly breeze sprung up, we would save our precious pennies and visit instead a sweet shop. Most sweets retailed at four ounces for 2d, and shopkeepers would painstakingly weigh out one ounce of each, at the request for 'A ha'pennyworth of raspberry drops, and a ha'pennyworth of chocolate chews, please', pouring them into tiny paper bags, or blue sugar bag paper, twisted into a cone shape. The few ounces of sweets which remained at the bottom of the jars were mixed together, and placed into somewhat larger bags, with the addition of a small novelty, a brooch, ring or tiny celluloid doll. These ha'penny and penny 'Dover bags' were extremely popular, as they often contained remnants of the more expensive sweets, hazelnut creams and sugared almonds, normally beyond the reach of our slender pockets, but which my father brought home on Saturdays as a special treat.

On regatta days, stalls selling streamers and confetti took their place alongside the fruit stalls and ice cream barrows. The rolls of streamers and bags of confetti were eagerly snapped up by the local youths, who proceeded to pursue the girls, stuffing handfuls of confetti down the backs of their dresses, accompanied by shrieks of protest; many a romance had its beginning in those far-off regatta evenings. Seaplanes armed with nothing more lethal than bags of flour would 'bomb' the assembled yachts and small boats, while the older inhabitants sat on deck-chairs listening to the band playing in Granville Gardens (later destroyed by enemy action). Roundabouts were set up for the children, while others made use of the roller-skating rink.

In those far-off days, at about four o'clock, regular as clock-work, a man would throw on to the beach scraps of fish for the seagulls, who would swoop down, their mental clocks alerting them to the time for their daily treat, some minutes before the man, presumably a fisherman, appeared on the scene. With the advent of war, the seagulls, driven from their home in the cliffs by the terrifying roar of the guns, made their way into the town, where, uttering their mournful cries, they build their untidy nests in the rooftops, splattering cars and occasionally the inhabitants as well, with their indiscriminate target practice. Happy as I was to visit home, now that the country was at war, I was nevertheless thankful to return to the comparative safety of Lords Field where, if the hours of work seemed long, I was sustained by thoughts of pay-days, and the planning of what I could afford to spend and how much could be spared to post into my little green savings book in preparation for my next visit to the coast.

I had been in Hampshire for almost a year to the day when my sister went into a nursing home in Twyford to await the arrival of a new baby. I use the term 'nursing home' in the loosest possible sense. Owing to staff shortages, the cleaning and washing (by hand) of mountains of nappies and baby clothes were carried out by those who were still 'ladies in waiting' and the food was frugal to say the least. To visit her meant a journey for Charlie, her husband, and me, involving three bus changes; although the home was clean and in pleasant surroundings, it was obvious that the patients were not enjoying a rest cure.

We managed to buy a few buns and apples to take in to my sister and, while we were there, she was able to rest and chat to us. My brother-in-law was frantically searching for more convenient lodgings, as their single room was totally unsuitable for the expected new arrival and Mrs Brown had appeared rather dismayed at the idea of a baby in the house. He managed at last to find for rent an old house at Freefolk, a pretty village two and a half miles from Overton, with picturesque thatched cottages.

The house was the lower one of three, which lay at right angles to the road, and the river flowed by a few feet from the door. In spite of its old world leaded windows this house, or to be more precise, cottage, was far from picturesque and boasted no modern plumbing.

Water, which often contained fresh water shrimps, was drawn from a pump in the earth-floored kitchen, and the bucket toilet in the outhouse was emptied twice weekly by local health authority employees, who drove an evil-smelling cart which called at a surprising number of houses for this purpose. The stench preceding its arrival lingering long after the cart itself had left was unmistakable. The villagers, like the Greeks, had a word for it.

My brother-in-law, greatly relieved to have found somewhere to live, however lacking it may have been in modern conveniences, travelled to Dover to arrange for the transfer of furniture and household items from their abandoned home and set to work to make the place habitable. When, after her three week stay at the nursing home, my sister arrived with her new baby boy, she was horrified on being shown round her new home, to see bats hanging upside down from the rafters in the outhouse. Primitive though it was, she too was thankful to have a place of their own again and invited our parents to stay for a short respite from the bombing and shelling and to see their long-awaited grandson.

The day which had been arranged for the christening dawned grey and cold. I was to be godmother. For the hundredth time, I glanced out of the window as the wind sent heavy-laden clouds scudding across the ominously darkening sky. Having stacked away the last of the dinner plates and tidied the scullery, I hurried with the other girls to the staff bungalow. My shoes, polished to perfection the previous evening, stood neat and gleaming and my clothes were arranged in my under-bed locker.

I had decided, it being a winter christening, that of my two coats, the 'London tan' square shouldered 'swagger' would be the most suitable. Although my hair was usually worn loose and tied with a ribbon bow on top, à la Deanna Durbin the young forties singing star, I did possess a hat, a dark brown straw 'pill-box', with a tiny veil, and half a dozen even tinier orange flowers. It was, strictly speaking, a summer hat, but as one always wore both hat and gloves to church in those days, it would have to do, I thought, especially as it matched my shoes, bag and gloves.

I discarded my overall, washed and changed quickly, and arranged the hat over my not too recently permed curls. Had I been blessed with a modicum of commonsense, or even a plastic carrier bag, I would, in view of the threatening weather, have tied a scarf over my head and placed the hat in a bag until I reached the cottage. However plastic bags had not been invented and the brown string handled paper carrier bags which most shops had offered for a penny had a disconcerting habit of disintegrating in a heavy shower, leaving one grasping two pieces of string and endeavouring to retrieve from the pavement the scattered purchases, clutching them to one's bosom in the brown, soggy remains of the said bag. In the absence of either sense or bag, I bade the girls 'cheerio' and made my way to the village bus stop. The drizzle which had commenced while I was dressing turned into a deluge even before I reached the camp gates and I squelched my way to the village. It was a wretched, bedraggled young godmother who left the bus at Jerry Lane and descended the steps to the cottage, carefully arranged curls hanging straight and dripping, with the centre of the pill-box reaching for the sky. My sister helped me out of my saturated ensemble, and I arrived at the church feeling self-consciously conspicuous in petrol blue 'Robin Hood' hat and matching coat reaching almost to my ankles. The simple and beautiful ceremony was performed without any further mishap and I hurried back to the camp to carry out my evening duties, leaving my wet clothes to be collected on my next visit.

Regarding my lengthening, straggly locks, I did some mental arithmetic, and decided to have my hair permed at the local hairdressers. The fifteen shillings (75 pence) which was charged for this somewhat lengthy procedure represented almost a week's wages. Prior to the introduction of the 'cold perm', the instruments for torturing one's hair into waves and curls appeared daunting to the first time client, whose hair, having been washed, thoroughly dried and trimmed, was then divided into tufts, on to which were slotted flat rubber insulating discs; each rubber washer having been deftly placed at the hair roots, the client, resembling nothing so much as a droopy-quilled porcupine, awaited the next stage of the operation. Pulling on rubber gloves, which had seen better days but would be difficult to replace in view of the shortage of rubber, the hairdresser then proceeded to wrap each tuft of hair in a small paper sachet impregnated with an eye-watering, ammonia based solution, rolling each in turn on to a heavy cylindrical curler.

This procedure completed, a fiendish contraption, on which the 'brain-machines' of modern science fiction must surely be based, was laboriously wheeled to the hapless client's side and each curler slotted into hollow cylinders which hung from wires on the perming machine. Having plugged in and switched on the current, the sorcerer's apprentice would place on her client's knee an assortment of magazines, then leave her to 'bake' for the time specified for her particular hair type.

Alone in her cubicle, the client could only try to concentrate on the out of date magazines or watch in the mirror the spiral of steam which wound its way to the ceiling at each alarming hiss and crackle from the machine, wondering if, when at last the wires were disconnected, her hair would go with them. Sinking ever deeper into the rexine covered upholstery under the weight of upwards of forty curlers, it felt rather as one tends to shrink within one's self as the dentist wields his drill.

What would happen in the event of an air raid, I wondered, would the hairdresser unslot each curler from the machine, or merely switch off the power, leaving the helpless client 'strung up' in every sense of the phrase? Considering myself fortunate in not discovering the answer to that question, my hair was finally unhitched, all in one piece, if it can be described in that way, the tight corkscrews washed, saturated in setting lotion and set into finger waves and pin curls. Then after another session under the noisy drier, having spent four tortuous hours in the pursuit of beauty, or at least, manageable hair, I emerged, face and scalp a glowing shade of deepest beetroot, contemplating that that was that for another nine or ten months. On reaching the camp, the stiff corrugated waves which had formed under the hairdresser's skilful fingers were vigorously brushed into a softer style. I was now ready for whatever the winter had in store, be it hail, snow or blow.

The winter was long and cold. We were thankful to finish work for the day, close the curtains in our quarters and shut out the night. One dry, but bitterly cold evening, in the break between tea and supper, the cry 'Fire!' was heard above the soft music drifting from the wireless. We grabbed our coats and hastily unearthed our gas-masks, thinking that incendiary bombs must have dropped from an unheard plane. Remembering our seldom practised fire-drill, we heaved from the hooks outside the bungalow, one between each two of us, three of the sand-filled, dome-bottom red fire buckets and, gas-masks slipping from our shoulders into the sand, made our way down the steps, in the general direction of the shouting and smell of smoke. Everyone, it appeared, had taken possession of a fire-bucket and they leaned, where they had been thankfully dropped, at every conceivable angle.

The boys had been hastily shepherded out of the dormitories and stood in straggling, chattering columns. Masters and male staff peered and threw buckets of sand under the raised assembly hall, from which poured clouds of choking smoke. It later transpired that Arthur, our young fire-raiser, presumably to relieve the tedium of long evenings cooped up in the dormitory, had decided to enliven the proceedings by building another fire under the said hall. Fortunately for all concerned, there being more smoke than flames, it had been speedily discovered and extinguished and a tender part of the young miscreant's anatomy was warmed by the application of the dreaded stick.

4: The Author outside the staff bungalow

Spring was welcomed by all; the longer evenings, particularly with double summer time, when the clocks were put forward in two separate stages in the interests of daylight saving. This move was not altogether popular with the farmers who complained that cows could not tell the time and could not be expected to alter their milk-producing habits, although it did enable the farmers to work late in the evenings to bring in the precious harvest. However it meant also that the youngsters could once again roam through the green countryside and strains of boyish voices could be heard drifting across the fields. Chalk, which had adhered not unwillingly to our cleaning cloths in the cold, damp classrooms of winter, now resisted every manoeuvre of the dusters and rose in clouds, settling in our clothes and hair, as we dodged the russet-coloured crane flies hovering in the dusty shafts of sunlight. The classrooms were out of bounds to the boys while cleaning was in progress but one young lad called in one warm sunny evening saying that he was leaving the next day and planted a kiss on my cheek, to the amusement of the other girl who was helping me dust and replace the honey-coloured chairs under the tables. I had to put up with plenty of teasing after that and, even more so, when a card arrived at Christmas with just my christian name on the envelope.

Chapter Three

PHANTOM COWS AND RIVERS OF BLOOD

THE GIRLS FROM THE VILLAGE often entertained us with their versions of local folklore. Part of Freefolk, where mists rose from the river beyond the trees, was reputed to be haunted. Margaret related to her enthralled audience that many years ago, in Cromwell's time, battles had raged in the area, and a path which branched off from the main route to the village, known as The Lynch, had, in days gone by, become a river of blood. She had, on certain evenings, while walking back to the camp, experienced a sensation of something warm swirling round her ankles. She was quite sincere about this and who was I to scoff at the tales of this quiet mannered, sensible girl? The Lynch was a very pleasant lane, with a row of charming thatched cottages, fronted by well-tended gardens. The trees which almost met overhead formed a welcome shade from the summer sun and, in autumn, the fallen leaves made a crackly, red-gold carpet. At night, though, it took on an entirely different aspect.

When I visited my sister, we often chattered at such length that I found, after waiting in vain, that I had missed the last bus back to Overton. On one of these dark nights, listening to the eerie hooting of the owls, I braced myself for the two and a half mile walk along the sparsely populated road to the village and from there to the camp, via The Lynch. My tiny electric torch, dimmed as per regulations with a scrap of blue paper, was of very little comfort. The oddly shaped trees and mists rising above the river beyond the trees played tricks with my imagination and it was not difficult to believe that those swirling shapes were figures from the past. The night air was still, with not a breath of wind, and walking quickly, with my heart beating fast, I was certain that I could hear deep, regular breathing. I turned; there was no one in sight, but still came the sound, slow and even on the night air. There was very little traffic in those days; even for those who could afford the luxury of a car no petrol was available, priority being given to doctors, and red coloured commercial petrol for those in business, the majority going to keep the armed forces mobile. No friendly lights appeared to make me feel less alone, dimmed though they might be. 'There are no such things as ghosts,' I told myself, but what other possibilities were there? Sleeping troops, perhaps, or diddycoys, the local name for gypsies? There was nothing to indicate the presence of either of these. The moon shone down on the unlit road and, walking quickly, I darted glances in the direction from which the sounds were coming. As the hedges thinned, I saw through the wire fence dark, squatting shapes which turned out to be nothing more fearsome than . . . sleeping cows!

My relief knew no bounds but there was still well over a mile to go along the path slightly elevated from the tree-lined road; then I had to pass the house with the blood-stained ceiling and walk up through 'the river of blood'. My panic increased with every step and I was certain I could feel the blood of long-dead warriors swirling round my ankles. Half walking, half running, I arrived thankfully at the bungalow to find the lights out and blackouts drawn back, but the door fortunately unlocked. I promised myself that never again would I miss that last bus. When I related the story to my sister on my next visit, she, of course said that I should have gone back and stayed the night at the cottage, and caught the first bus back in the morning. In spite of my good intentions, I often found myself waiting for the already departed bus. On one occasion, when a barn owl flew silently by like a white, airborne ghost, a huge army transport lorry pulled up and a voice with an American accent drawled, 'How far're you goin', lady, do y'wanna lift?'

Now we all knew what happened to girls who accepted lifts from strange men and I wanted to say 'No', but thoughts of ghostly mists, phantom cows and rivers of blood ran through my mind. I just could not face that long, eerie walk and I did not want to put my sister to the trouble of finding me a place to sleep at that time of night, so, throwing caution to the winds, I ventured, 'Could you give me a lift to Overton, please?'

'Sure,' said the seemingly disembodied voice. A tall man in a smart American uniform swung down and helped me into the front seat perched above the huge wheel and sat on my left, while another voice greeted me from my right, telling me to move along, as there was plenty of room, The one who had helped me climb aboard started up the engine of the left-hand drive truck and said that they were on their way to pick up servicemen from a dance in the village. Any fears I may have had vanished as the two perfectly charming American coloured men chattered in their engaging southern drawl, singing snatches of *Stardust* and, on reaching Overton, one of them insisted on escorting me right to the gates of the camp, where he wished me a courteous 'Goodnight, lady.'

I found it difficult to convince my brother, who was just setting out to look for me, that his little sister was not on the downward path to ruin. He signalled with a raised little finger, the sign deaf people use for 'bad'.

The old cottage which my sister and her husband now occupied had a fairly large walk-in pantry, with rows of shelves on which were stored crockery as well as food. The pantry door would not stay open of its own accord, so a heavy pastry board was used to wedge it open while things were being replaced after a meal. One day Charlie prised open a trapdoor which was in the floor of the pantry. Some four or five feet down on the chalky mud floor we were somewhat perturbed to see a number of bones of varying shapes and sizes. He replaced the trapdoor, speculating as to the origin of the bones and how they came to be there. The house, they learned, had been formerly occupied by an old man who had recently died. It had been condemned and only let for rent because of the influx of people from other areas. I nursed a mental picture of an old man sitting by the open trapdoor, discarding bones from his dinner. Was that how they came to be there, or was there a more sinister reason for their presence? We never found out, but one day when the pastry board fell down, and the door slammed shut while I was putting some plates away, I got out of there mighty quickly, much to my sister's amusement.

Quite apart from the presence of the bones, there were happenings which intrigued me, appealing to my sense of the dramatic. I sometimes stayed at the cottage overnight when Charlie was on night shift and have pleasant recollections of light summer evenings spent in the garden picking huge, whiskery pink gooseberries, listening to the ducks as they floated lazily by on the slow-moving river – and of hauling out my adventurous nephew when he slipped in as a two year old. Later I talked with my sister in the soft double bed, watching as the moon cast shadows on the sloping wall of the pink-washed bedroom; the eerie 'hoo-oo-hoo' of the white barn owls with the slow flapping of wings heard distinctly through the open window, conscious, too, of the creaking and settling of the old cottage as the wooden beams which had absorbed the heat of the sun's rays contracted in the coolness of the night. The scarcely heard noise which could have been a light step on the stairs and the inexplicable falling open of the rope-handled door leading to the sitting room where the black-leaded stove gleamed from my sister's constant labour with brushes and emery cloth.

There was an old gas stove in the kitchen-cum-scullery and a gas lamp in the living room, candles being used to light one's way to bed. During the hot weather, the fire was left unlit, the sun's warmth being sufficient to dry and air the washing.

'You be up early this morning, missus,' said old Turk, my sister's neighbour from across the patch of grass and plantain which separated the two rows of houses. My sister was surprised, she was a fairly early riser, but Turk, as everyone called him, rose at four-thirty some mornings to cycle to his work some distance away. He explained that he had seen smoke rising from the chimney early that summer morning. My sister was puzzled, the fire had remained unlit for almost a week.

'It must have been next door's chimney,' she said. 'I don't light the fire when it's warm like this.'

Turk pointed to the chimney and my sister stepped on to the patch of grass and looked up. Sure enough, a thin spiral of smoke was threading and weaving around the chimney, her chimney. The fire remained unlit for the rest of the evening and, related my sister to me on my next visit, she and Charlie made several trips out of doors to look at this strange phenomenon. Charlie had to attend for his home guard duty that evening and, feeling a little uneasy at leaving his wife alone, he went to the bedroom and examined the wall behind which the chimney passage lay. As he suspected, it was warm, and decided to call the Fire Brigade on his way to the village.

'It often happens in these old houses,' said one of the firemen. 'The walls and chimneys are plastered with cow dung and they often smoulder for days.'

They concluded that there was no real danger, but with a minimum of mess injected a squirt of water into the offending chimney; when, before going to bed, my sister examined the wall, she discovered it was still warm. The strange thing was, it continued to smoke for several days, and my sister almost convinced herself that the place was haunted. I was interested to see, on one of those lovely country programmes shown on our independent television station, that the area is now Watership Down country and the pub which was then called *The Jerry*, giving rise to the name Jerry Lane opposite where the cottage stood, is now called *Watership Down.*

When they had become settled in their new home, and the area remained quiet, they arranged to bring their little girl, who was by then nearly seven, back from Wales, and their family was once again complete.

A number of the boys at the camp had come from a home, Hollybrook, so although those fortunate enough to have a home and family to visit went home for Christmas, the camp of necessity had to remain open to cater for these lads. A skeleton staff of masters remained and during the Christmas period, we did only that which was barely necessary to keep things ticking over. The same could not be said of the chefs, who, despite growing shortages, excelled themselves and provided an excellent seven course Christmas dinner; soup, turkey and all the trimmings, Christmas pudding, mince pies, locally grown fresh fruit, cheese and biscuits and coffee.

This was followed by a social evening, to which, among other friends of the staff, my sister and Charlie were invited.

Male and female quarters being side by side, it was, of course, an unwritten rule that each keep to his or her particular bungalow, except for our twice weekly cleaning sessions when girls in twos or threes gave the men's quarters a thorough dust and polish, all the men being responsible for their own bed-making and sheet changing. The only visits to our quarters by the men was for repairs, or when beds were moved in or out to adjust to the ever fluctuating staff numbers.

I mentioned earlier that our doors were never locked during the daytime and one night during the Christmas period, when the dining hall had been decorated with holly and trimmings, we returned to our bungalow. After the usual chatter, we prepared for bed, turned out the lights and opened the blackout curtains; a series of agonised yells burst forth as we climbed into our respective beds and found that each contained a large sprig of holly. A scamper of feet was heard outside and the door of the adjoining bungalow was quickly closed behind those responsible for our discomfort, who had apparently been listening for our reactions to their unwanted gifts of festive greenery. We, of course, retaliated in our own special way. The next time we entered their quarters for a cleaning session, we went armed with needles and cotton, and while one girl, ostensibly cleaning windows, kept a look-out, the others, of whom I was one, sewed up the bottoms of pyjamas from some beds and turned up sheets halfway to make 'apple pie beds' on others, so that in order to get in, beds had to be stripped and remade. Real *Girls' Own* stuff! Honour satisfied, we crouched in the sitting-room late that night, listening to the sounds of chaos from next door, as the men, on that cold and frosty night, stripped and remade their beds and unravelled our delicate handiwork.

Kent has always been known as the Garden of England but Hampshire is equally deserving of that title. We often went for walks on fine days during our afternoon breaks, along the old Roman road, or to the old mill at Southington, where the tall trees were reflected in the still, clear water; and into the village itself, where fences near a factory which produced kapok-filled goods were hung with drifting gossamer strands. The cool, clear watercress beds, where the tangy green plants swirled into lazy, ever-changing patterns were in direct contrast to the parched, cracked earth of summer, from which the sun appeared to have drawn up every drop of moisture.

Mr Davies, leaning on a convenient gate, could often be seen keeping a paternal eye on his young charges.

I had often noticed an unpleasant, indefinable smell permeating the otherwise pleasant atmosphere; a companion, in answer to my query as to its source, pointed through the hedge, where, at intervals hung straggly, rotting rat carcases. Apparently the local council, in an effort to keep down the ever-increasing numbers of these vermin, paid out twopence for every rat's tail presented to them and the village lads – and no doubt some of our boys, too – were quick to take advantage of this lucrative source of income, as every fence I glanced at was, I noticed, similarly arrayed. It was a pity, I thought, that they could not devise a more hygienic method of disposing of the carcases.

Rats were not the only pests with which we had to contend; we were terrified of the bats which on summer evenings seemed intent on scaring the wits out of us. We didn't know then that, owing to their in-built 'radar' system, the chance of being hit by them was remote, but old wives' tales of having to cut out a wildly fluttering bat if one became entangled in one's hair prompted us (after making certain that there was no one else in the lane and in the absence of a protective scarf or cardigan) to pull our skirts over our heads and run until we reached the camp. Then, recovering our decorum and with one eye still on those dratted bats, we smoothed down our dresses and walked sedately into the safety of the bungalow.

5: Kathleen and Vera with some of the boys

But for sheer nuisance value, it would have been difficult to find a worse pest than the earwigs which abounded everywhere; we could hear them creeping in the wooden walls and, after discovering some in our beds, we all, in the 'earwig season' of summer, meticulously stripped and searched our beds before climbing in. Even then we imagined that they were crawling over us in the blacked-out room, which they probably were, as we often found the odd one or two when making our beds after breakfast. They even got into the enormous steam-heated boilers in which the food was cooked. Cabbage that had been washed and prepared in readiness for the next day was found to contain any number of the pests, so the kitchen staff had to take special precautions to prevent it happening again.

It is often said that one tends to remember only the sunny days of one's youth. That is in part true, for I can remember clearly the extremes of very hot summers, or cold winters when snow made the surrounding countryside breathtakingly beautiful, and have only vague recollections of running from buildings with coats flung over our heads, through pouring rain, as we performed our many and various duties. Having lived all my young life in a seaside town, I had, before the seafront was tank-trapped and cordoned off during the war, spent many a happy hour on the beach, as you will have read earlier. There were no such facilities in Overton, but there was the river Test. So I, with pretty Dot from Dagenham, flame-haired Vera and Kathleen who had recently arrived from Southampton, wrote home for our bathing suits. When they arrived, we put them on under our dresses, and with rolled towels containing undergarments under our arms, went down the lane to Bridge Street, where, behind a sheltering hedge, flowed the coolly inviting river. Apart from the odd tin can which had escaped the recycling bag, there was none of the large-scale dumping so prevalent today and we revelled in the coolness of the water which was marred only by the sharpness of the pebbles.

Our carefully chosen spot turned out to be not so secluded as we had imagined, as passersby, drawn no doubt by our squeals, peered at us through the hedge with expressions ranging from mild amusement to stern disapproval at the antics of 'they evacuees'. The villagers, though, as a whole, bore the invasion of their pleasant rural retreat with extreme patience and good humour; and when I was invited to the homes of my workmates I was treated very kindly and found the broad rolling 'r's of the older people's accent fascinating.

On one of these glorious summer days, when a travelling fair set up outside the village, we of course went to see what pleasures it had to offer. We strolled round the sideshows. For a charge of twopence a time we went on the roundabouts and were thrilled to see the old-fashioned swing boats. We climbed in, two to a swing and Myrtle, who lived in the village, pulled the gaily coloured ropes, sending the swing higher and higher. Too late I remembered that from a very early age, anything with a swinging motion caused me to suffer terrible feelings of giddiness and nausea. I tried vainly to suppress the rising feeling that I was about to lose my dinner, when Myrtle, noticing my decidedly green face, managed to slow down the swing and helped me off. Never had the road back to camp seemed so long.

Browsing in Howard's, the shop-cum-library, one day, a book with a blue and white cover depicting Dover castle and the harbour caught my eye. It was Alice Duer Miller's *The White Cliffs*. Of course I had to buy it, although the 2s/6d (12.5p) which I paid for the slim austerity volume upset my budget for the week. Although the story barely touched on the white cliffs, I wallowed in pure nostalgia as I read the story of the American lady who lost her titled English husband in the first world war.

Most of the land around Overton was owned by Lord Portal, as was the paper mill. Henri de Portal, a Huguenot refugee of the early eighteenth century, had devised a way of watermarking banknotes which made forgery difficult. In 1724 he won a contract with the Bank of England and built the imposing Laverstoke House, midway between Overton and Freefolk. Lady Portal, in her cloche hat and low buttoned, straight-cut coat reminiscent of a 1920s photograph, was a familiar figure in the villages and made regular visits to her tenants, who now included my sister and her husband. Lord Portal's team regularly played cricket against one formed by his employees at the mill, of which Charlie was a member. Watching the leisurely game played in such a pleasant rural setting, it was difficult to believe that there was a war on.

About once a year, Mr and Mrs Davies entertained Lord Howarth, who was one of the governors of the National Camps Corporation. Waiting at table was one of my least favourite duties, as I was inclined to shyness, but on these occasions, as one of my duties as manager's maid, I was required to wait on him and other guests in their bungalow. The mere thought of waiting on a real live lord had me shaking in my shoes but he put me quite at ease, enquiring about my home town and I almost forgot my shyness.

The large dining hall was periodically oiled by the male staff, both to preserve and disinfect the wooden floor. The thick pine-scented oil was well brushed in, but it took several days to really penetrate the wood, and one day, when it was my turn to wait at the masters' table, my heel skidded on a particularly oily patch, and the plate of tomato soup which I was about to place in front of one unfortunate master landed instead in his lap. I handed him the serving cloth and beat a hasty retreat to the kitchen, vowing never to wait at table again, but chef had other ideas and insisted that I continue serving the meal. With my face as hot and red as the spilled soup, I returned to the dining hall and, with shaking hands and acute embarrassment, served the next two courses. My own schooldays were not too far behind me and I was still inclined to regard schoolteachers as a race apart.

There were seldom less than two hundred boys at the camp, nearer three hundred was the average number and the food, although not quite up to the standard of that which the staff enjoyed, was good and wholesome; but one day when, as was the usual practice, the chef dished up a dozen or so platefuls which stood on the hotplate to start the queue moving when the boys arrived, we were horrified to see white eyes floating in the rabbit stew. What could have caused this lowering of standards, I can't imagine, unless in an over zealous economy drive they had decided to include the heads with the rest of the meat. May, who came from Llantwit Major, one of those who came with Mr and Mrs Davies when the camp opened, refused to add vegetables to the plate, saying she was not going to serve *that* to the boys; we, feeling revolted by the sightless eyes rolling round the plates, endorsed her views. With the arrival of the boys imminent, chef, displaying a rare flash of artistic temperament, sloshed the stew back into the heavy container, and stomped back into the kitchen. Not daring to enter his domain, we heard a flurry of activity and brusque orders issued. When, with a minimum of delay and an expansive beaming smile, he presided over a first course of spam, cabbage and mashed potatoes, no one suspected that the meal was a hasty substitute. We could not help but admire the chef's resourcefulness, for what was, after all, a very uncharacteristic lapse of standards. The pigs, at least, lived well that day.

The kitchen, with its huge central cooker, topped by a shining steel hotplate, the steam heated boilers and rows of plum duff moulds, was a hive of activity. The chefs, Glyn Thomas from Wales, and Peter Tramm, who was of Italian extraction, were normally cheerful and ready for a joke. It was only when things did not go entirely to plan and utensils were banged down harder than was absolutely necessary, that we considered it wise to keep at a respectable distance. The dapper little Italian chef, who had worked in a top London hotel until bombing had made it no longer tenable, lived with his glamorous dark haired wife in the village. When we girls were making tea, or performing some duty in the kitchen, he would say, 'Here, try this,' or 'What do you think of that?' Mock cream was one of his specialities and scraping out the container after he had filled his icing bag was a sought-after privilege. Among his other much appreciated delicacies were salmon slippers, which were jacket potatoes, the insides scooped out and whisked with scarce pink salmon to a fluffy smoothness, and piped with mashed potato to simulate a white, furry top. These, though, were only for the staff; the boys, who should have had first consideration, were served much plainer fare.

The turf-covered mound which was the top of the staff air raid shelter was, owing to its secluded environment, a favourite spot for sunbathing in the summer. Although in the main it was so quiet that there might not have been a war on, there were occasions when the siren did sound, and we would all troop off to the shelter, accompanied by Mr and Mrs Davies and, of course, the beloved Shaun. It was only at these times that our gas-masks, which normally lay forgotten in our lockers, saw the light of day. These were very informal gatherings and we would sit on the benches, talking of things in general, some of us seizing the opportunity to get on with knitting jumpers, gloves or pixie hoods with whiskery, off ration knitting yarn. Even though there was no sign or sound of danger and jobs remained unfinished, we were not allowed to leave the shelter until the all-clear sounded.

Although the bungalows were centrally heated, with radiators in the sitting room, and pipes running the length of the room behind each bed, we all enjoyed, in winter, the extra comfort of a hot water bottle, which we filled from a kettle in the kitchen.

Owing to wartime shortages, rubber bottles were unobtainable, the only ones being made of glazed 'stone'. One night chaos reigned when, pushing the cooling bottle away with my foot, it fell to the floor with a resounding crash. It took some time to convince my sleepy room mates that their rude awakening was due to something as innocent as my warm-hearted, if cumbersome bedmate, and not, as they had fearfully imagined, a bomb. We often lay awake listening to the dull thud of bombs, thankful that we were not on the receiving end, our hearts going out to those people who were having yet another disturbed night.

I had been to Southampton on one of my free days with Lily and Charlie and my nephew; the devastation we encountered made me feel thankful that at least the boys in our care were being spared this horror.

Like Canterbury and Dover, it was 'business as usual', with shopkeepers and staff cheerfully carrying out their services to the public in tarpaulin-covered cellars. An added touch were the American sailors in their white uniforms and doughboy hats; just like in the films, we said.

I was kept awake for some nights for reasons other than air raids, a nagging toothache, which, in spite of taking aspirins and, on the advice of one of the staff, sticking a clove (supplied by one of the chefs) in the cavity, became more and more painful. Mr and Mrs Davies with their usual concern, decided that they would take me to a dentist in Basingstoke on their weekly trip to the bank.

Having rung and made an appointment, they kindly settled me into the back seat of their cream coloured car (I clearly recall the registration number, FLU 920) for the nine mile drive and, after waiting until the offending tooth was pulled, left me in the car while they called at the bank and made several purchases. It was my first visit to the dentist. The cocaine injection which the dentist had used for the extraction of the tooth seemed to affect my left side from jaw to ankle; when, after two hours or so of immobility in the car I tried to walk, I felt as if I were doing a passable impression of a wooden soldier. Mrs Davies packed me off to bed and sent for Nurse Jackson, who, brisk and white coated, drily pronounced that I'd live, thinking, I'm sure, that I was 'swinging the lead'. Needless to say, my circulation speedily returned to normal and I was able to continue with my duties, free from toothache.

I have no recollection of paying the dentist and my employers, I'm sure, did not deduct his fee from my wages. I thought nothing of it at the time, but they must have paid him as there was no national health service in those days. With the advent of rationing, sweets, as I remarked earlier, had become virtually unobtainable, began to flow again into the shops, and the twelve ounce monthly ration was eked out over three weeks. Our weekly visit to the cinema was made even more enjoyable with a quarter pound bag of toffees to salve our sugar-starved palates, but on the fourth week, our coupons exhausted, it was back to austerity again.

Such avid filmgoers were we, that if there were two films showing at different cinemas that we wanted to see (and this was invariably the case) we would, keeping to a very tight schedule, take in both shows on the same day, leaving just in time to catch the last bus. Often, though, our carefully laid plans, as is so often the case, went awry. There being very little else in the way of entertainment, queues formed outside most cinemas and we had no option but to stand hopefully in a queue which appeared to stretch for miles, waiting for the commissionaire to announce 'room for one more', as we waited patiently to laugh at the zany antics of Abbott and Costello, travel yet another 'road' in the amusing company of Crosby, Hope and Lamour, or to escape to Hawaii, where girls danced the hula in grass skirts and were joined by Betty Grable, Don Ameche and John Payne as they feasted under the swaying palms, while an invisible orchestra played as they burst into song in the inevitable love scenes, romantic, but not explicit. The patrons received very good value for their shilling, in the stalls, or one and nine seat in the circle, as each programme consisted of two films, plus short films made by the Ministry of Information dealing with subjects ranging from hints on saving gas, coal, electricity and water, to recipes for austerity vegetable pies from the Ministry of Food for those days when, because of rationing, meat was not on the menu. Pathé Gazette, the newsreel and magazine programme, heralded by the familiar music and crowing cockerel, showed scenes of fighting abroad and heroic rescues by Civil Defence workers at home, always ending on a cheerful note, fashions for the ladies, a song by Peter Dawson, or some item of comic interest which might help dispel the gloom and keep up the morale.

The lavish Hollywood musicals, the throbbing Latin American music, the outrageous towering head-dresses of Carmen Miranda, who appeared to have fashioned the entire contents of Covent Garden market into a gravity-defying piece of millinery, the cinema provided escapism for the entire family; parents and children alike forgot for a few hours the austerity and shortages as they relaxed in the comforting semi-darkness.

British film makers offered comedy and stirring sagas of war on land, sea and in the air, all guaranteed to lift the heart and make us proud to be British, while in the interval the organist, rising magically from the depths, entertained us with tunes old and new. One night, my timing amiss, I was just in time to see the dimmed tail-lights of the last bus leave the depot, and there was no alternative but to search for a taxi, At a shilling a mile, and the shilling tip which I felt was obligatory, the ten shillings which were to last until next payday were swallowed up on that nine mile ride.

A later visit to Basingstoke with Jenny also resulted in reaching the bus depot some minutes after the departure of the bus. Having spent our few shillings on shopping, tea and our shilling seat in the stalls, we couldn't rustle up the price of a taxi between us, so there was nothing for it but to walk. With my loquacious Welsh room-mate as a companion, the trek was not as daunting as it would have been unaccompanied; it even appeared something of an adventure. We passed a blacked-out village with white-painted fences and a humpbacked bridge, and the bus stop where the conductor always called out 'Winkleberry Lane', but I remember little else of our nocturnal journey through what was then a mainly rural area.

On reaching the bungalow in the wee small hours, we were greeted by cries of, 'Where have you two stop-outs been? We were just about to organise a search-party!' As the girls who were still awake appeared to have settled down for the night (and who could blame them?) this seemed unlikely. We fell thankfully into our beds with only the briefest of explanations and had to endure good-natured banter as to the state of our morals for many a day after that marathon walk.

One evening something happened that was, to us, almost as exciting as anything that the cinema had to offer. Jenny and Margaret had joined me in the sitting room where I was ironing; the iron, plugged into the adaptor on the light hanging from the ceiling, caused the shade to play a rattling accompaniment to the music on the wireless. During the news bulletin it was announced that a high-ranking German official, Rudolph Hess, had made a lone flight to Scotland and landed by parachute, breaking an ankle in the process. The purpose of his flight was to negotiate peace terms. Surely, we thought, this must mean that Germany was losing the war? Even the name Rudolph could have come from a list of characters on the wide screen. When it transpired that he had been taken prisoner and nothing was to come of what we regarded as an heroic attempt to end the war, we felt almost cheated.

A great deal of publicity heralded the debut of Wilfred Pickles as the first BBC newsreader with a regional accent; although his northern accent was not as pronounced as in his post war series *Have a Go*, it was, nevertheless, a departure from the strictly observed BBC English favoured at the time and was, no doubt, another attempt to personalise the announcers so that they could be distinguished from any 'fifth columnists' who may have taken over the airways in order to give false information to the listening public. We occasionally tuned in to Lord Haw-Haw, his mocking pseudo-British accent exaggerating British losses in both human life and battles; his attempts to lower morale were met with equally derisive comments and profound disgust that someone whom we believed to be British could act in so treasonable a manner.

'Auntie BBC' was a model of decorum and nothing was broadcast that could be described in any way to be in bad taste.

Jack Warner had made the words 'blue pencil', denoting censorship, into a national catch phrase; it was blue pencil this and blue pencil that, allowing one to substitute one's own expletives, which, lacking as we were the doubtful benefits of the adjectives which flow all too freely from the television these days, were mild in the extreme.

There was still no news of my room-mate's young man. She looked up expectantly each time the mail was handed out, only to be disappointed yet again. No news of my brother, either. A regular soldier, he had spent the six years prior to the war in India, sending home many snapshots and parcels of beautifully crafted Indian brass and silk and velvet embroidery; had the not war intervened, he would have completed his seven year posting in 1940.

While cleaning the masters' commonroom one crisp spring morning, I attempted to shuffle a pile of newspapers into some semblance of order. A picture of a smiling young soldier leading a column of troops through a village 'somewhere in the Middle East' caught my eye. I was certain that it was my brother. Back home, my mother had seen the same photograph and wrote expressing immeasurable relief that my brother appeared, at the time the picture was taken, at any rate, to be safe and well. It was not until he arrived home in 1945, after serving in many areas of combat and finally in Burma, where he was awarded the British Empire Medal, that we discovered that the picture my mother had cut out and treasured was not of my brother, after all. I sincerely hope that the smiling young soldier whose photograph afforded my mother some degree of comfort survived to return to his own family when hostilities ceased.

Overseas mail did often, for obvious reasons, get held up, and letters which had been so eagerly awaited sometimes arrived in batches, usually in the familiar green envelope which informed that the contents were liable to censorship if anything which could have been even remotely useful to the enemy was inadvertently penned by the sender. We were almost as delighted as our friend, when, as we had assured her so frequently would happen, two letters arrived for her by the same post. It was a happy day, indeed.

I was looking forward to my next weekend at home. My mother had written to say that she had met an old school friend of mine and had invited her to tea on the Sunday. When Thursday arrived, I knelt by my bed, transferring the things I would need from my under-bed locker to my suitcase, ready for a quick get-away the following evening. This is a moment in time, now and real, I thought, but it will never come again.

Above the rattle and clackety-clack of the train as it snaked its way along the shining rails that Friday evening, I could hear the thud of bombs and the sound of aerial combat. I stifled the almost over-whelming urge to lift the corner of the blind to see how near were the bombers; nervously studying the faces of my fellow travellers, I felt that we were hurtling, unseeing, into destruction, well aware, particularly on this night when the 'bombers' moon' shed its silvery glow over the landscape, that the train with its billowing cloud of steam made an easily recognised target. A soldier began to sing the words of a popular song of the day, *Roll out the barrel,* and the chorus was taken up by his companions, until the entire carriage and surrounding corridors resounded with the deep male voices.

Unnerved at first that I could no longer hear what was happening outside our sealed cylinder, I gradually relaxed and was relieved to find the atmosphere quiet and peaceful when the train drew to a halt at the next station.

'What a bit of luck, what a bit of luck,' enthused a trio of young airmen, as they boarded the now emptying carriage, thankful to divest themselves of their cumbersome luggage, gas mask and 'tin hat', and commenced a conversation punctuated with references to 'Wop A-G's,' what they thought of 'Flight', humorous anecdotes of various 'erks', and various phrases alien to my uninitiated ears, which set me trying to decipher the strange language of these 'Brylcreem boys'.

I finally concluded that 'Wop A-Gs' must almost certainly mean 'wireless operator air gunner', when my deliberations were interrupted by the arrival of my train at its destination.

On leaving the train I found that there was an alert on, so I was directed with the other alighting passengers to the air raid shelters. Almost immediately could be heard the unwelcome sound of falling bombs and rat-tat-tat of anti-aircraft fire.

'Ah well!' said one of the servicemen, 'No need to worry; if it's got your name on it, that's it, and you won't know anything about it.' The all-clear sounded; it was just a short alert, a stray bomber jettisoning his bombs before crossing the channel, no doubt. Case in hand, I left the station and made my way home. Mutilated stumps of garden railings, once lovingly painted a glossy blue, green, black or maroon had become dulled with the passing of time. No longer sharp and gleaming from the onslaught of the men with the hacksaws, they rose from the low cemented walls outside the houses like memorials to a lost way of life. The public had given generously and unstintingly of their ornamental gates and railings, in fact any metal which could be melted down for munitions, and gaps on many a kitchen shelf showed that even the humble aluminium saucepan had been called up and sacrificed to build planes that would guard our skies and hit back at the enemy.

It was obvious that my mother had gone to a great deal of trouble to prepare tea for us on the following Sunday. Precious 'points' from her ration book had been used to purchase a tin of pink salmon; always the gardener of the family, she had sacrificed some of the flowers in her small garden to 'dig for victory' and there was crisp green lettuce and spring onions; she had made a blancmange with powdered milk and a spice cake containing dried egg, sweetened with golden syrup, (also on points), accompanied, of course, by slices of off-white National bread.

It has been said that we, as a nation, were at our most healthy during the war years, with our carefully planned rationing system, which may well have been true, but how we longed for some variety to our monotonous diet and looked forward to the days, in the hopefully not too distant future, when we could once again enjoy real, crusty white bread. How ironic that the large combines now saturate the market with tasteless plastic slices far inferior to the bread we grudgingly accepted then, squeezing out of business the small family bakers who supply mouth-watering 'real' bread.

We waited well past the usual time for tea, but there was no sign of Joan. 'Strange,' said my mother. 'She said she was looking forward to seeing you again.'

I found myself thinking, 'If it's got your name on it . . .' and somehow I couldn't do justice to my mother's carefully planned meal.

The next day we heard. The house where Joan had lived with her parents in Glenfield Road had suffered a direct hit. The bomb had had their names on it. Mercifully they would have known nothing. You never heard the one that hit you.

After tea that evening I walked slowly to a place that was, and still is, a favourite haunt of mine, a sloping meadow known as Whinless Down. It is a lovely spot, completely bordered on one side by hawthorn bushes, which, for a few short weeks in May and early June, are shrouded in white May blossom; in September, juicy blackberries, mingling with the scarlet berries of the hawthorn, are to be had for the picking.

I sat on one of the benches where a young soldier who had been billeted with us for a few months at the beginning of the war had carved his initials. The old Norman castle, rising proudly above the trees in the distance, overlooked the stretch of water between here and Calais as it had done for centuries. The beautiful words of Matthew Arnold's *Dover Beach*, which we had learned at school (could it really have been only three years ago?) came into my mind.

> The sea is calm tonight, the tide is full,
> The moon lies fair upon the Strait.
> On the French coast the light gleams and is gone.

The cliffs of England stand, glimmering and vast
Out in the tranquil bay.
Come to the window, sweet is the night air,
Softly from the long line of spray
Where the sea meets the moon-blanched land.
Listen, you can hear the grating roar of pebbles
Which the waves draw back and fling,
At their return, up the high strand.
Begin and cease, and then again begin,
With tremulous cadence slow
That brings the eternal note of sadness in.

Dover beach, which had seen the miracle of Dunkirk, where, as in other nearby ports, the little ships had returned with their precious human cargo; where it had seemed, after all, that God was on our side, calming the waters as the wounded landed on our friendly shores, where trains and buses waited to bear them away to recuperate and re-assemble; and where, battle-stained but proud in defeat, the uninjured marched through the town, directed not too harshly by their sergeant, 'Heads up now, bags of swank!'

'By, it's gre-ee-at to be home!' said one dishevelled but smiling young warrior, whose Geordie accent proclaimed his home to be far north of here; but the small group of onlookers knew exactly what he meant to convey. He was home, safe on British soil at last. He was one of the lucky ones. There were so many of his comrades who had not survived the perilous journey and row upon row of blanket-clad bodies were given temporary sanctuary in many an old, silent building, one of them being the old market hall, adjacent to which light anti-aircraft guns on the roof of a public house were aimed at any approaching hostile aircraft.

The wheezing, sinisterly comical note of a cylinder feeding the ponderous barrage balloons in the grounds of the Boys' County School, (now Grammar School), below me broke into my thoughts. The pupils had been evacuated to Ebbw Vale even before France's 'grand old man' Marshal Petain had conceded defeat and now the grey and red brick school, with its white fortress-like turret was occupied by the Women's Royal Naval Service (the Wrens) and the green plush playing fields were being churned into furrows by the service vehicles from which the huge grey aerial elephants were suspended. To those of us who lived in the vicinity it was a familiar sound to which we awoke, always supposing that 'Jerry' had allowed us to sleep at all. The long grass around me rippled as a breeze sprang up and a blackbird in search of his evening meal regarded me warily.

I shivered. The moon would soon be shining fair upon the Strait. The bombers' moon. At Cap Gris Nez the guns might already be primed to send their deadly hardware hurtling in our direction.

Behind me, where buttercups had grown tall and spindly in their efforts to compete for their fair share of daylight among the purple-tipped grasses, were five craters where the naked chalk lay exposed and raw, the salvo of bombs having barely missed the school. Would I, would anyone, be spared to see again the sunlit fields of spring, buttercups and daisies shining white and gold in an earth-bound milky way?

Would the wild roses bloom with no-one to see their fragile beauty among the green hawthorn berries? The white bindweed which curled among the nettles had already furled their white umbrellas against the approaching night. The enemy was too close for comfort. I almost ran the half mile down the lane to the safety of home. For Joan and her parents the night would hold no more fear.

My mother looked at me and understood as I packed my case in preparation for the morning. The night was noisy with the heart-lurching drone of heavy bombers and sporadic bursts of ack-ack fire, but we emerged from the shelter to a brilliantly golden day, the sky clear and blue, as if to compensate for the destructive elements which had lurked in the concealing darkness of the night.

Chapter Four

FOUR-FOOTED CASUALTIES

WITH THE LIMITED NUMBER OF CLOTHING COUPONS AVAILABLE, silk and rayon stockings were treated with all the care their scarcity demanded and, in winter, we wore the more durable ankle socks, or bobby sox, as our American counterparts called them, where 'bobby soxers' were swooning over the young Frank Sinatra. We wore our neatly darned stockings like a badge of honour and, if we were unable to be as well dressed as we would have wished, we at least endeavoured to keep our clothes clean and well pressed.

Having read that stockings kept better in screw-topped airtight jars, we enquired if chef had any to spare; glass itself was a scarce commodity, when every jar or bottle was put out for collection, the inch-wide labels were removed from tin cans and everything put into separate boxes for recycling. This became almost a religion and one came near to believing that the omission of one small label or tin from its appropriate box would be tantamount to sabotaging the entire war effort. By salvaging everything that could be put to good use, switching off lights when leaving a room, and adhering strictly to the recommended five inches of bath water, we were doing something positive to help. Paper bags were carried when we went shopping and used until, like fine old lace, they literally fell apart or had to be discarded for reasons of hygiene. Wrappings were kept to the bare minimum; there were none of the present day battles to extract products too well-wrapped.

Buses displayed cartoon posters of soldiers in the desert gasping for water, imploring the public not to waste so precious a commodity. Newspapers seemed to grow progressively thinner. We followed the adventures of the *Daily Mirror's* Jane and her pet dachshund, Fritz, and read of the new wonder material, nylon, which, it was claimed, was sheerer than silk, but many times stronger. Stockings made of this fabric would outlast ordinary stockings by as much as a month. (Whatever happened to this wonder material?)

When our carefully hoarded stockings became no longer wearable, we bought permanganate of potash which could be mixed with water to create shades ranging from pinky beige to deep copper. When our mixture had reached the desired shade, we would sponge it over our legs and feet, drawing a dark pencil line down the backs of our legs to simulate the seams of the fully fashioned stockings which were popular, when obtainable. This we found far superior to the bottles of 'liquid stockings' which were on sale, as the colours didn't run in the rain and could only be removed in the aforementioned five inches of bath water. I have since heard that gravy browning was used by some people, but I can't believe that it was as effective as our little concoction.

At regular intervals everyone was required to register at a local office, in alphabetical order and according to the year of one's birth. There was in existence what was known as 'direction of labour' and if a person had been doing a certain type of work, he or she could only be employed in that particular field. Of course, young men, on reaching call-up age were, by this means, certain to find a buff envelope marked OHMS on the doormat within a few weeks of registering. Everyone had an identity card, without which no ration card or insurance card could be issued. On visits to Dover, having written to obtain my permit, I found that there were various check-points manned by the army and out of town buses were stopped while the identity card of everyone on board was checked.

In May, 1940, the Local Defence Volunteers (which became the Home Guard) were formed and, on certain evenings and at weekends, one could see bands of men, too old for call-up or in reserved occupations, drilling, often with only broomhandles and staves, learning unarmed combat for the defence of their homeland in the event of invasion. They were eventually issued with rifles, some of them relics of world war one and, in spite of good humoured references to their being 'England's last hope', this Dads' Army did a valuable job, releasing enlisted men for other duties.

The easily recognised Lysanders, with their spatted wheels and wings which reminded me of insects, were often seen in the fields adjacent to the camp performing what can best be described as hedge-hopping, but we were all more than a little concerned to see on one occasion planes and gliders disgorge literally hundreds of white and coloured parachutes nearby. In Battle of Britain days, the familiar white parachutes floating down from damaged planes were an all too common sight, but these coloured chutes in such profusion were an entirely new innovation and we half expected to hear the church bells peal out to warn us of imminent invasion. After viewing the colourful display from our vantage point in the broom cupboard, work temporarily forgotten, we thankfully came to the unanimous conclusion that it was just another exercise and it would not, after all, be necessary to call the local campanologists out of their enforced retirement.

The coming and going of staff continued, although we had a fairly permanent, compatible nucleus. Three girls and a middle aged woman arrived from Ireland and the older woman was assigned to work in the kitchen. One day, while slicing bread on the machine, she was unfortunate enough to cut the tip off one of her fingers. The blood lay in pools on the floor. One of the chefs padded and bandaged the poor woman's finger, before Mr and Mrs Davies drove her to the hospital. It was all too much for Bill, one of the male staff; normally robust and cheerful, he collapsed in a dead faint. The next time he teased me for my lack of inches ('she drew herself up to her full height, three foot six'), I was able to retort, 'At least I don't faint at the sight of blood.' When staff members dwindled to a degree which made the wheels run less smoothly (and threatened to put our free weekends at risk), ladies from the village were called in on a part time basis.

One of these was Dolly, a good lady of incredible bulk, who seemed oblivious of the teasing remarks directed at her by our male colleagues. She did her ponderous best but squeezing past her plump figure in the limited confines of the kitchen whilst balancing a precariously tottering stack of flat bottomed dinner plates was comparable to negotiating a roadway roundabout with an insecure load.

Another of these ladies suffered frequent attacks of bronchitis, aggravated, no doubt, by her addiction to 'the weed'. Uttering sympathetic noises, we strove not to laugh while, beyond her vision, those same male colleagues, hands clasped to their chests, bent double and silently gasped in simulated agony as, surrounded by a permanent haze of cigarette smoke, she informed us of the current state of her 'bronichals', coughing and wheezing while stubbing out yet another 'coffin nail' in the nearest available receptacle, be it ashtray, saucer or sink-tidy.

'Sorry,' she would say, all concern, when we finally collapsed into fits of choking, 'I'm givin' up after this packet,' but the seemingly bottomless packet somehow never became empty.

The scullery afforded an excellent view of the long drive and in late summer and early autumn, boys, hands clasped across strangely bulging shirts, could be seen making their way to the dormitories. I assumed they had been swimming in the river and, perhaps because such a pastime was forbidden, were hiding their towels inside their shirts. It was many years before I discovered just what those mysterious shifting bundles really were.

Sometimes, when beads of perspiration stood out on our faces as we struggled with the mountains of crockery from the last meal of the day, one of the girls would collect 8d from each of us and, off duty at last, return with small bottles of cider from the Red Lion. Feeling wickedly decadent, we sipped the cool, golden apple juice and listened to local ghost stories.

The second winter I spent at Lords Field was particularly cold. Situated above the village, we were exposed to the elements. 'It be too cold for snow,' said Mr Roberts, one of the courteous old workmen. Centrally heated as all of the buildings were, we felt the cold keenly, as, bundled into our coats, we went about our duties. When snow eventually fell, the camp was transformed into a sparkling fairyland; icicles hung from every window, and the snow was crisp and deep underfoot. Boys and staff were set to work clearing pathways and grey and white mountains appeared alongside every building; someone suggested a snowball fight after duty that night, male versus female staff. We sewed up our scarves to make pixie hoods and put on our oldest gloves. While we were pandering to our creature comforts, our opponents had been busily engaged in building stocks of ammunition which also served to shelter them from our sporadic attacks and we were well and truly routed; at last, with rosy cheeks and tingling fingers, we trooped off to the kitchen and warmed our fingers on steaming cups of cocoa.

The entire countryside took on a picture postcard atmosphere; the road to Freefolk which appeared so menacing at night was a delight to behold with trees on either side of the road festooned with snowy white lace. The green and white footbridge which spanned the road at the ineptly named Rotten Hill was overlaid with sparkling cotton-wool and icy pendants which shone like diamonds in the sun.

When winter passed, my sister invited our parents to stay for a short holiday. When the time came for my father to return home to start work, they persuaded my mother to stay longer, as they felt that a break from the continuing raids and shelling would do her good and she could help look after the growing baby.

Rex, who was the son of Floss, my childhood pet, had, as a six week old puppy, been adopted by Lily and Charlie, but given into my parents keeping when they moved to Hampshire. He was small, well behaved and rather timid; of course he too was invited to stay.

One bright spring afternoon, when I went to visit them, I took Rex for a walk back along the road which led to Overton. He was, as I said, very well behaved and usually walked 'at heel'. The strange place and tantalising smells of the countryside, however, got the better of him and he hared off up the bank to disappear among the trees. When he failed to reappear, I became worried and called and whistled to him. It was then that I heard a blood-curdling yelping and howling, which did not stop although I continued to call. Thinking that he must have been attacked by a larger dog, I scrambled up the almost vertical bank and grabbed a piece of wood, hoping to scare off the other dog, if dog it was. There was no sign of Rex, but I pushed through the thick bushes in the direction from which the dreadful cries were coming, and at last I saw him, his eyes wide, with the whites showing in terror, his front paw trapped in an iron jagged toothed trap, about a foot wide, and secured by a chain which was embedded in the ground. I had no idea how to release him, I was afraid that if I touched it I would only cause him more pain, so I ran through the woods, hoping to find someone who would help me. I heard a crackling of twigs and saw a man; almost in tears, I told him what had happened. In an entirely emotionless, matter of fact manner, he freed Rex and, thanking the man, I somehow managed to scramble down the bank and carry the injured animal back to the cottage. He limped for a long while after that dreadful walk that had started out so happily, but he lived on to the ripe old age of sixteen, when, in 1946, too tired to leave his basket, or even to eat, my parents regretfully decided it would be kinder to end the life which had become only a burden to him. My brother carried him out on his way to the vet and, on reaching the gate, Rex lifted his tired old head as if in a last gesture of farewell.

The traps were, no doubt set to catch foxes or perhaps rabbits to eke out the meat ration, but I would dearly have loved to see the person responsible for so much suffering, not only to Rex, but any poor unfortunate creature unlucky enough to fall foul of his cruel gadget, ensnared in his own trap, unable to free himself, awaiting the arrival of someone, anyone, who would release him.

Rex was not the only casualty that year. The beautiful Shaun, after several hours of concerned vigil by her devoted mistress, produced a litter of four kittens, sired, no doubt, by the handsome black tom from the headmaster's bungalow next door, or a visiting village moggie. They became, as days went by, enchanting bundles of multi-patterned fluff, giving me the minimum of extra work, thanks to the fastidious attentions of their ever watchful mother.

At the rear of the bungalow work was being carried out by builders, involving piles of sand, cement and the mixing of concrete. The kittens, growing more beautiful and inquisitive as time went by, were anxious to explore the world outside the limited domain of the kitchen and I was devastated to learn, one morning, that one of them had been crushed by the heavy boot of an apologetic workman when it ventured on to the wooden verandah outside the kitchen; extra care was taken of the three surviving kittens and they were all later sent to good homes, my sister's being one of them. Their progeny now, I shouldn't wonder, form a sizeable part of the local feline population.

The derisive songs of the early days of the war, *Run, rabbit, run* (the only casualty, it was reported, of the first bomb to land on British soil was a rabbit killed in the Scottish highlands) and *We're gonna hang out the washing on the Siegfried Line* (German defences) kept the British spirits high; the song did its bit to help diminish the enormity of the power which threatened to overcome all of Europe.

It has often been said that times of trouble can be gauged by the silliness of the songs of the day: *We're poor little lambs who have lost our way,* sang the American pilots and *Mares eat oats and does eat oats, and little lambs eat ivy* asserted the vocalists of the popular dance bands.

Our enthusiastic, if not always tuneful renderings of *Tangerine, Marie Helena* and other songs which rang out daily in the BBC Light Programme's *Music While You Work,* backed by the rumble and swish of the dishwasher were not always well received. There were requests to tone it down a bit. Subdued by the lack of appreciation of our efforts, a temporary lull ensued but youthful exuberance and girlish high spirits could not be dampened for long; quietly at first, then louder above the clatter of the white ironstone crockery, the kitchen and dining hall echoed again to the songs which, to this day, when given an airing on the radio, transport me back in time to that red tiled kitchen.

Chapter Five

THERE IS A HAPPY CAMP

IT SEEMS THAT ONE HAS ONLY TO SWITCH on the television or pick up a newspaper these days to hear of yet another instance of the increasing violence and vandalism among some, and I do stress *some,* of today's youngsters, a sharp contrast to those days when the boys of Lords Field, even if they were not absolute angels (and what boy is?) were, in spite of the absence of everything which modern youth regards as essential to life, as well behaved as anyone could expect a boy to be.

Having written of life as it appeared from the staff side of the hotplate, it occurred to me that I knew very little of the boys' activities at the camp, apart from the organised games, rambles and the effort they put in to caring for the sheep and garden. What of the boys who tried to reach home, individually, or in the 'mass breakout'? They must have had many a tale to relate to their families when the war was over and no doubt relived it all in the telling to children of their own. No chronicle of those days could be complete without the co-operation of the boys themselves.

A letter quoting the camp song, asking for anecdotes of those days, was duly published in the *Southern Evening Echo* and I was gratified to receive letters, not only from Southampton, but from various parts of the country, as cuttings were sent by relatives to the widely scattered former evacuees. As Barrington Little wrote, reading my letter 'was like having an immediate replay of my early life condensed into two paragraphs of print'.

In spite of the very strict discipline which is remembered, they all, without exception, agree that at times the cane may have been used a little too liberally. Nevertheless, 'It was,' to quote Bill Lynn, 'expected and accepted with no thoughts of future "aggro", and the discipline helped give them the confidence to face the future.' A thought, surely, for all those do-gooders who suggest that 'violence breeds violence'.

The stories of life in the camp and when, together or separately, they decided to leave to find out how their parents were faring made exciting, humorous and often touching reading. A clear picture emerged of the strict, military type of discipline with which the camp was run, aimed at creating self-sufficiency among the young inhabitants, which began shortly after the outbreak of war, when schools in Southampton, as in other parts of the country, were closed, even, it was rumoured, 'for the duration'.

The joy of the pupils at this indeterminate holiday was short-lived when it became known that boys from the various centres of learning were being sent to a 'safe area' and the masters who elected to become part of the scheme faced the formidable round the clock task of moulding youngsters in their formative years into a well adjusted, self-reliant community.

On reaching the camp, speculation having run rife during the journey, many of the young travellers were disappointed to find that it was not a camp in the true sense of the word. Dreams of a boy scout existence with songs round the camp fire vanished like the smoke they would have engendered as they entered the camp gates, but if they had heard the adage that 'it is better to travel hopefully than to arrive', they soon tried to settle down to their new way of life.

'The morning bell,' wrote Barry Little, 'ringing out loud and clear heralded the start of each school day, when the dormitories became a veritable hive of activity, as the boys washed or showered, made their beds, very correctly, and generally tidied their respective "dormies". Great pride was attached to the state of these six long buildings and there was almost fanatical competition among the occupants for the shiniest floor and best-kept interior.' He continued, describing how, with true British grit and the gift of making the best of a bad job, the task of polishing the floors was undertaken to the enjoyment of all concerned. 'Every Tuesday, before school, we had to move the beds to one side, and polish the other. This was done by two small boys sitting on a blanket, and two boys pulling, after the polish had been applied to the floor. Then the procedures were reversed. Believe me, at the end of the task, the floor shone like glass and heaven help anyone who went through with shoes on.'

The occupants of Dormitory Four were equally inventive when it came to making light of hard work, although one hopes that there were not as many casualties as the writer of the following narrative suggests.

'The floors were polished on Saturdays by teams of small boys, who pulled mops bound in dusters across the floor, complete with ballet in the form of small boys clinging to mopheads. Many years later we were to remember the scenes of carnage caused when bodies flew off with centrifugal force, reminiscent of the chariot race in *Ben Hur*.' – This from Robert Flather in Norwich.

Having restored a state of order in their respective dormies, the boys paraded in the 'square' and, as I observed earlier, latecomers were given a taste of 'the dreaded stick'.

As Bill Lynn commented, 'I was only late once; believe me, that cane really hurt on a cold morning.'

After breakfast classes commenced as in a conventional school and in the evenings the boys were left very much to their own devices, writing home, playing chess or draughts, and employing their skills at handicrafts. 'Chalk that could be found in abundance was carved by young sculptors into a variety of shapes, miniature heads, animals and slippers, to be presented to admiring relatives on visiting days,' wrote Colin Douglas from Burton on Trent.

Chalk carving became a cottage industry; oddly mis-shapen heads that had once been a piece of chalk plucked from the grass came to life under the gradual whittling of a budding sculptor. Peep shows were constructed from boot boxes, with three dimensional scenes glued therein, and covered in tissue paper; cigarette cards changed hands for a view of the contents. Mouth organs and Jew's-harps provided music in those pre-transistor radio days, and whips sent wooden tops spinning in competition. Inter-dormitory raiding parties crawled under the raised buildings and the young warriors carried out their mock battles in the long grass.

'The dormitories were erected on piles driven into the chalky subsoil, leaving a rabbit warren of explorable byways beneath the floorboards. Many an hour was spent crawling in the half-dark with white knees and peering gaze, across the disputed territory beneath another dormitory.'

'Bundles of compressed grass deftly fashioned into the size, shape and almost the consistency of cricket balls would volley and thunder to the imminent danger of the marauding hordes of attackers; often the field would be swept clear by a hedge-hopping Beaufighter from a nearby store frigate or shore-based naval station. Instantly small boys would disappear beneath mounds of hay, cackling like machine guns, and lobbing a barrage of grass to the skies.

'On dark winter evenings the mock battles and "commando raids" were carried out with the advantage of complete darkness and hostages and prisoners were taken from opposing dormitories; these same dormitories often echoed to the subdued sobs of the homesick, or to the unmelodious harmonica playing of budding Adlers.

'The boys came equipped with a wide repertoire of backstreet skills; the various abilities of being able to hobble three feet off the ground on stilts; to spin tops with deft flicks of leather thongs. Other skills were cultivated by some and taught to others on a barter system: "I'll teach you to whistle through your fingers if you'll teach me the mouth organ." "Lend me your penknife to carve this lump of chalk and I'll let you borrow my Jew's-harp."

'Handicrafts were also in evidence; woodwork is remembered with some cause for pride of craftsmanship, if only for creativity that was evidenced in the preparation of a matchbox holder, fashioned out of two small blocks of wood; due to an error in making out it failed to operate; its preparation had consisted of four weeks of evening work, it was three or four times its intended size when finished, innumerable tools were broken and a knuckle carved into a scar which can be seen to this day.

'I hope I won't make you shudder when I tell you that rats, lizards and grass snakes, in precisely that order, are what I remember most about leisure time at Lords Field. Cruel little devils that we were in those days, we used to beat the haystacks with sticks, then run and hide, waiting for the rats to come out; there were literally hundreds of them and we would throw stones at them, keeping a wary eye open all the same, as we had heard that rats, when cornered, make for one's throat. The lizards and snakes we would find under bits of old tin or wood in the fields or sunning themselves on a wall or under a bush. Tins and jars were in short supply in those days; we would save any that had been brought to us on visiting days and, when empty, save them to keep our "pets" in. One day we managed to persuade chef to give us a seven pound stone jam jar and we must have had at least a dozen of each squirming around in it. We fed them by swatting flies and mosquitoes that were on the dormitory windows, swatting them with rolled up comics. I well remember how we were in awe of the lizards' tails which wriggled about on the floor, when the poor creatures shed them in an effort to escape our attentions. When some of them died we let the rest go but we couldn't resist the temptation to catch more when the opportunity arose.

'Scrumping was one of our favourite activities. Like most boys, we didn't consider it stealing, not when there appeared to be so many apples lying around just for the taking; we ate as many as we could (we always seemed to be hungry), then filled our shirts and smuggled them into the dormitories. Many's the tummy ache I suffered from eating green, unripe apples and hard small pears. There was a place near the railway lines where you could pick wild strawberries; lovely, they were, but the best ones were over the fence and on the railway bank, well out of reach.'

The mystery solved, at last, of all those strangely bulging shirts! Although in my letter to the paper I quoted the camp song *On a hill above a valley*, it would appear that the following song, sung to the tune of *There is a happy land* is the one most associated with the camp; it was quoted in many of the letters, with alternative words in brackets.

> There is a happy (lousy) camp far, far away,
> Where we get bread and scrape (jam) three times a day.
> Ham and eggs we never see, sugar is a luxury,
> We get sawdust in our tea, three times a day.

South of the border, You are my sunshine and all the Glen Miller songs are guaranteed to evoke a nostalgic memory these many years later, but one which is perhaps peculiar only to the erstwhile inhabitants of Lords Field is also recalled:

> The king called this morning,
>   We had to be drastic,
> We bought her a dress
>   That was made of elastic.

Sports nights were a regular part of the evening routine and helped in dispersing youthful energies; but, as Bill Lynn recalls, one was often called upon to knock hell out of one's best friend, with some reluctance, in the frequent boxing bouts and the opportunity to let off steam on a less favoured opponent seldom presented itself, while one master compelled his young charges to run to the flagpole at the bottom of the field and back to the dining hall before supper, the last boy reaching that spot having to forfeit the meal.

Young Ronnie was rather a tubby lad who was invariably last but Bill and a couple of friends decided that a sturdy, well built lad such as he

72

needed his nourishment and they contrived to be last, encouraging the puffing youngster to reach his goal. Red faced and triumphant, young Ronnie sat down to supper that night, but Bill and his two well-intentioned friends not only forfeited their evening meal, but received 'six of the best' for not trying.

The boys' physical well-being was left in the capable hands of Nurse Jackson and queues formed outside the sickbay for the monthly medical, any cuts and sprains being promptly attended to with the brisk, but kindly, admonishment to take more care in future.

The annual sports day, when the sun shone brilliantly down on the young athletes, is recalled with pride and on organised rambles, the older boys, one of the letters informed me, contrived to lag behind and cut lengths of the creeper adorning the trees into strips, 'which had the taste of a strong cigarette', indulging in their first tentative leanings toward the dubious delights of smoking, putting paid to the dreams of many an aspiring young post-war Olympic contender. Hunting and fishing were indulged in somewhat surreptitiously but young David Hampton and his friends caught a trout which would have been the envy of fishermen with far more sophisticated equipment than the string and bent pin baited with bread which lured the hapless fish from the calm waters of the river Test; but, fearing that they had broken some local byelaw by so doing which would in turn incur the wrath of their master, they sold it to the local fishmonger for the then princely sum of two shillings.

Young Bill and his friends, while on one of these rambles, caught a large rabbit which they proudly presented to one of the chefs; next day tasty rabbit stew was enjoyed by all, I suspect with the addition of some hastily procured bunny from the local butcher. Miracle man that Bill proclaimed him to be, chef would be the first to admit that even he could not stretch one rabbit to feed the five thousand, (or in this case, three hundred), but was, I feel sure touched by the boys efforts to help eke out the rations.

Mr Wandlass, voted a 'great guy' by Bill and his friends, accompanied the boys on many of these rambles; he was very well liked and was still visited by many of the boys in his retirement from teaching. The rambles did not pass entirely without incident; Colin Douglas recalls that one master, taking them on a birds' nesting expedition, showed the boys some interesting nests. He said that he would climb up to see if the nest in one tree was being used and if there were any eggs in it. If there were more than three eggs, the boys would be allowed to take one. The master reached a height of about twelve feet from the ground, recalls Colin, when the branch broke and he fell to the ground 'with such a thud. We all stood back wondering what we could do for him, he just lay there for about fifteen minutes and then got up. I'm sure, thinking back, that he must have hurt himself.' Hunting was not confined entirely to wild life. There were, for boys, prizes in the form of bomb splinters, shrapnel, pieces of parachute, and even the top of a propeller from a crashed Spitfire, which must have been a problem on cleaning days, until the dormitory master had a blitz of his own and disposed of the treasured relics.

Colin and his friends decided that, to help the war effort, it might be a good idea to collect waste paper. Bill Lynn's older brother, John, who sadly died at a young age, was Colin's best pal and went with him. They called at a large house, which Colin believes was owned by Lord Portal, and asked if he would lend them a wheel-barrow. The gentleman said he hadn't a barrow but would lend them a pony and trap. He must have had second thoughts about the pony, but lent them the trap undeterred. The patriotic boys thanked the gentleman for his kind offer and took turns between the shafts.

'We must have collected tons of paper,' said Colin, 'and we thought that in some small way we were contributing to the war effort.'

Pet rabbits which were kept at the rear of the dormitories fulfilled the need for living creatures that the boys could call their own and which in normal circumstances would be satisfied by a dog which would take part in their boyish excursions.

Young Colin was extremely proud of Streaky, his ten pound Belgian hare, which thrived in spite of the noise of three hundred boys in full cry. While some boys tended the sheep and vaguely remembered cows and a goat, aspiring young apiarists cared for bees which yielded a fair amount of honey.

A rare treat for the older boys was an evening visit to the old cinema at Whitchurch, accompanied by a master – 'It had to be a suitable film, of course.' How the younger ones envied them, especially as the favoured ones returned well after the normal lights out. On Saturdays, all the boys were allowed into Whitchurch for the afternoon matinee at the cinema. In those less affluent days they often walked the four miles each way to save money. With the pennies thus saved, they satisfied their healthy young appetites with fish and chips from the village chippy, (a bag of chips cost 2d. and fish was 4d.). One day, having received a number of complaints from the local people that the boys were buying up all that the proprietor could fry, Mr Collins threatened to put the village out of bounds unless they drastically cut their consumption of this tasty addition to their diet. The boys, not wanting to put their cinema trip in jeopardy, reluctantly agreed to accept his conditions and contented themselves instead with the tantalising aroma which wafted from the shop selling the forbidden fruit.

The village bakery was extremely popular, a new loaf warm from the oven could be purchased for 2d; hacked into rough slices and liberally covered with jam or chocolate spread brought by the eagerly awaited visitors, it, too, helped supplement the often uninteresting diet.

Ah, yes, the visitors: what bittersweet memories the word evokes. 'Sunday, of course,' wrote Barry Little, 'was the great day of the week. Visitors meant comics, chocolate and more food and, best of all, to see one's mother or relations. I remember as if it were yesterday standing on the verandah of Dormie 3 (a perfect vantage point for viewing the road up from Overton) and watching with growing excitement for the first glimpse of the Summerbee coach that brought the precious cargo. This was always a very emotional time, because not all boys had visitors; luckily I always did. Oddly enough, directly they arrived you began to dread the moment coming when they had to leave. Inevitably the dreaded moment came and that was it for another fortnight; one crept into a corner, feeling very sad and far from home.'

Wrote David Hampton: 'Parents and younger brothers and sisters could visit on occasion. Little is known of the journey they took; to the ten year old inmates such visitors appeared under the hot summer sky of 1940 as if they had dropped from it. One boy's sister, these many years later, remembers being given a miniature chalk shoe when she was three years of age.'

Michael Parker recalls, 'Jam, butter and Bemax were brought by our relations on visiting days and kept very safely in our lockers by the side of our double decker beds. We used to go to the village if we didn't have visitors. It was a very traumatic experience, being away from home. We'd perhaps go on a solitary ramble or sometimes a gang of us would play some game or other, not letting on how we felt, although we all knew, really.'

Mrs Jean Wilson remembers visiting the camp as a five year old. 'Thinking back I suppose it seems strange that I and a lot of the younger ones stayed at home, while older ones, like my brother, were sent to the so-called safe areas. I used to enjoy the visits, it always seemed to be sunny, childhood always was, I suppose. I know my mother would rather have had us all at home together but I suppose Brian was sent away so that he could continue his education.'

Mrs Elsie Mason was one of the first to reply to my letter in *The Echo*. Her son Donald, she wrote, was a former evacuee who had very happy memories of Lords Field and was now a very caring person, working in a Welsh hospital; in spite of the strict discipline it was a happy time for him and he received a very good education.

'Many a younger sister, now herself a mother, recalls visits to Mike's, Jimmy's or Alan's camp. I was three when my brother went to Overton and can still recall how excited I became at the prospect of visiting the camp on the bus with all the other mums, a few dads and young children. Sweets were hard to come by and I remember my mother scouring the shops for things to take to Jimmy. She often bought packets of five sweet cigarettes, not because she wanted to encourage him to smoke, far from it, but because they and liquorice sticks were some of the very few things that were off ration. I still remember the taste of them. It was a hard time for kids.'

Mrs May Davies recalls: 'We used to go and visit John on Sundays. I think several buses made the trip. I remember seeing huge, towering beds (bunk beds, really). On fine days we would go for a picnic and eat sandwiches my mother had brought with her. Quite unnecessary, really, because there was always tea provided at the camp. I remember there were haystacks everywhere in the fields near the camp. On wet days we would all go to the assembly hall. I seem to remember some sort of entertainment being put on.'

From Mrs Joyce Dyer: 'I remember going to see my brother when I was quite young. He was at the camp for most of the war. When the weather was fine we would go for walks in the village or in the fields. Sometimes we would just walk round the camp or sit on one of the white seats. The place seemed to be swarming with boys who appeared quite huge and grown up to me.'

From G. Bourne: 'My brother Tom used to show us the animals. There were quite a lot of sheep there, which seemed strange. He was, and is, a keen gardener and proudly showed us a patch of ground he and his friends had been cultivating. I think his interests in gardening had their 'roots' in Lords Field camp.'

Dorothy Ward recalls: 'We used to go on picnics; my mother packed sandwiches of cheese spread and dried egg, which wasn't too bad. We went through a fence where there were haystacks with boys sliding down and having a rare old time. I suppose I was a bit of a tomboy and, in spite of my mother's warning that the farmer would come and tell us off, I joined in and got my legs scratched by the sharp straw for my pains.'

Mrs Eileen Evans wrote: 'I remember going to see my brother. He used to stand near a sort of square where the bus turned round. He always became excited and showed off a bit. I am a mother myself, now, and realize it was because he was upset at being away from home and didn't want to show it. He, like my mother, was always near to tears when we left. Although they were hard days, I think we were a lot happier. We didn't have much in the way of treats and nothing like the toys and things that kids have these days. You were right when you said in your letter about the pressures being real in those days, but everyone seemed to pull together and I don't remember anyone getting into trouble.'

Chapter Six

HONESTY, AN INHERENT PART

IT APPEARS THAT I WAS RIGHT in my assumption that, in spite of the deprivation experienced in the war years, honesty was an inherent part of the boys' makeup.

'I can remember only one or two incidents of stealing,' wrote Barry Little, who sent several enthusiatic accounts of his days at the camp, 'and these were dealt with very severely, and *never* re-occurred.'

'We lads were no angels in those days,' said Bill Lynn, 'but, as you say, we were not vandals. There was only one instance of stealing that I remember, a boy who stole some sweets from a shop in the village and he was expelled from the camp.'

As I stated in the first chapter, I was fortunate enough to have arrived at the camp shortly after a near miss when bombs landed nearby, but some incidents which could best be described as hair-raising were experienced prior to my arrival, as the following quotes will show:

Bill Lynn continues: 'During the blitz, we would stand out in the field and watch the fires burning in Southampton, wondering whether our home and mum and dad were OK. Do you remember when a German bomber, being chased by a Spitfire, dropped his bombs intending them for the camp; they missed and exploded in the sewage farm next door? My brother Ginger and I were in one of the shelters when the bombs went off. I was flat on the floor, but my brother was standing up at one end and he ended up halfway down the shelter. We thought our dormitories had been hit, but we found out just what had been hit by the smell when we came out of the shelter – phew!'

'I remember going down to the shelters every night,' wrote Colin Douglas, 'and the night the school was nearly hit when we were watching the film, *The Thirty-nine Steps.*'

These raids and the certain knowledge that Southampton was being subjected to heavy bombing gave rise to the desire to get home at all costs. Colin continues:

'We were pretty determined to reach home. The masters were very strict in those days and you had "six of the best" if you didn't do as you were told. I may have been rather difficult in those days, but it seemed as if I had more than my fair share of punishment. It was after one of these canings that I, together with five other boys, decided to make our way to Southampton. We got together a few sandwiches and, armed with an alarm clock, set off. When we got to the fence, one boy decided he couldn't climb over, so we left him behind. We hadn't gone more than a few miles when one of us trod on a bees' nest, so you can imagine, we ran about the next two miles pursued by the bees. About ten or twelve miles from the camp we came across a crashed Wellington bomber that had just come down. The crew appeared to be alright and by this time it was fast becoming dark. We found a haystack in the corner of a field and tried to get some sleep; not long afterwards the sirens sounded and the bombers were coming over as usual; the gunfire and the bombers seemed to be coming close.

'I then began to think, "Have we done the right thing running away like this?" Things were getting pretty bad but, after a while, we began to walk on as we couldn't sleep. We seemed to have walked for miles and were getting hungry.

'Pretty soon after that, we came across a small station, I think it was either Sutton Scotney or Micheldever. We clambered up on to the platform in the pitch dark and found a long bench and we all sat down with our heads on each others' shoulders, dead beat. I was tapped on the shoulder by my friend, Chinky Andrews, who said there was someone coming with a torch. He shone it along our faces and asked what we were doing there at that time of night, we ought to be in a shelter. He took us to the station master's office; we were confronted by this rather fatherly figure who asked us what we were doing and where we had come from. We related our stories to him and he seemed very understanding. After making us a cup of cocoa (the best we had had in ages), he said he would put us on a train to Southampton if that was what we really wanted but he thought it best that we should go back to Overton, as everyone would be very worried. We decided to take his advice and he rang the headmaster. We had a long wait until he arrived.

'During the journey back going down country lanes, a Home Guard jumped into the road and hailed us with a "Halt, who goes there?" and the headmaster had to relate our story to him also. I remember there being tears in his eyes at this point. He promised to have a word with the masters who were hitting us so much and we all felt guilty at causing so much worry. We were looked after very well in those years; the shortage of food was felt by everyone at the time and we all seemed to pull together.'

Happily all ended well for these five lads, as fortunately it did for most of them, if one can disregard the cane and the occasional 'clump round the ear' dispensed by parents only anxious for their safety.

'Let me assure you that the railway lines weren't the best way,' wrote Bill. 'The best way was over the fence at the south side of the camp, then through the watercress beds, into Lord Portal's property, and with a few apples in our pockets, we were set for the long hike home. I remember the first time we ran away, it was on a Friday night. We were two miles outside Winchester and it was midnight, so we slept in an army pillbox for the rest of the night; a soldier came in, he was hitch-hiking back to his barracks and he gave us a bar of chocolate to share between the eight of us. We got home about ten o'clock on the Saturday morning and I was promptly greeted with a clip round the ear from my mother, who had been informed by the police that I had run away. I was sent back on the Monday; some of the lads had been sent back by their mums and dads on the Sunday and they had already been punished by the masters, which was twelve of the best on the back-side. The masters called everyone to the assembly hall to witness my punishment. My trousers were stuffed with paper; I was already for it, but my luck ran out. I had six of the best on each hand.

'I ran away several times, not because I wanted to, but other boys who were homesick wanted to go home. I knew that I would be sent back and I knew the punishment, but most of all I knew the way home without being caught. Only once did we get caught and that was with the police in a Black Maria. We ran from them and they never caught us but they shouted that, if we gave ourselves up, they would take us into Southampton. We decided to give ourselves up. At the time, we were taking home a young boy who had been badly beaten up by one of the masters and he was bruised all over his back; when we showed the policemen, they were only too pleased to take us into Southampton. There must have been some kind of report put in about it, for none of us got any punishment at all when we got back. I have no regrets about

Overton camp, we went in boys and came out men. Maybe if kids today had schools like Overton, I am sure they would be better off for it.'

Another writer, one of those involved in the 'mass breakout', recalls: 'I remember when the mass breakout came, I can only think it was done for devilment. There were the usual three of us and we decided to go with the rest. My brother didn't want to come with us, so off we went through the wire fence at the bottom of the field, running like the devil in our grey flannels and wellie boots. It looked as if the whole camp was breaking out. We didn't follow the railway lines but hared it off across the fields; I was glad of my wellies then. We passed Portal's mill and finally got to the white road out of Whitchurch. An army convoy came down the road and we stood there thumbing. Then the last lorry stopped and the soldiers asked us where we were going and we told them Southampton. We finally reached Southampton and we filled our shirts with apples which the soldiers had given us. When we got off the lorry, it was in the middle of an air raid. We ran down the road and got home. It had taken us less than four hours from the time we left the camp.

'While I was in the shelter with my parents, a policeman came to tell them that my brother and I had run away, but I told them that I had come by myself. We were taken back to the camp the next day, the three of us, taken before the headmaster and made to promise solemnly not to do it again. We had to laugh when my mate said, "I swallow my promise." We heard later that most of the boys had been caught within two hours, so we were quite proud to have made it home.'

Age was no bar when the call to home and parents made itself felt, Eight-year old Kenneth Jack and his brother covered the thirty miles by hitch-hiking and spent the last of their carefully conserved pocket money for the final stage of their journey on bus fares.

Some of them arrived to find their homes reduced to rubble. Paul Reader was one of these: 'I had been called to Mr Collins' office and told that my home was damaged; as a result, I was something of a celebrity among the boys for a while. It was not until I went to see it later, with the wallpapered walls of the living room and blue distempered walls that had been my bedroom exposed to the world, that the full extent of the loss hit me.'

James Warren also lost his home: 'I used to lie in bed at night and listen to the bombs being dropped on Southampton. I think most of us cried at times but the older boys teased us and called us cissies if we were seen to cry. I used to pray that my mother would be safe and my dog, dreading that I would never see them again.'

Michael Parker had been looking forward to his next visit home. His mother had promised that she would make him a birthday cake. He knew little of the planning that this reasonably simple effort would call for. The spoonful of sugar saved each week and put into the special tin. The giving up of a week's ration in favour of icing sugar (always assuming that this was available). The precious 'points' used for dried fruit; and mock marzipan which could be made from several unlikely alternatives, soya flour, potato powder, or stale cake crumbs, liberally flavoured with almond essence.'

No austerity magazine or newspaper worth its salt would consider itself complete without recipes using weird and wonderful ingredients to compensate for the lack of those that had become virtually unobtainable. Women's magazines abounded with recipes for 'warmalade', sugarless cakes and puddings, how to dry blackcurrants to use in those cakes and how the common marrow could be used to complement many a dish, even, with the appropriate flavourings, masquerading as pineapple or bananas and, of course, recipes for marrow jam.

Michael, like most males, knew little of the culinary cunning of the wartime housewife and merely wondered what his present would be. A train set would be too much to hope for. An annual, perhaps, of his favourite comic? Some additional units for his meccano set?

His mother arrived on visiting day, rather surprisingly, just a week before his proposed visit home. With forced cheerfulness she broke the news. Their home had been seriously damaged while she and his sister had spent the night in the shelter. The newly made but as yet un-iced cake had been among the 'casualties'.

It had often occurred to me that the boys were at risk when they went home on weekend visits and for the holidays. Was it really assumed that the bombers would take time off during these visits? Jimmy Warren was hoping to see his mother and grandmother on visiting day. He was fond of his gran. In the days before his arrival at Lords Field, he had spent many a happy hour in her neat little cottage. Grand-dad had been alive then and although times were hard and money scarce, gran could always be relied on to produce some home made cake and fizzy lemonade. The 'country' smells of the village, stewed blackberries and gooseberry pies always reminded him of gran, whose small garden boasted several fruit bushes.

He was surprised, therefore, to see his father, clad in the now familiar battledress step from the bus with his mother on visiting day. His delight at this totally unexpected visit turned to sadness when he learned that his father, who had been stationed up north, had been granted compassionate leave to attend the funeral of his mother, Jimmy's beloved gran, another victim of the nightly raids.

Peter Wright had heard of casualties among his friends' families and he had not seen his mother for several weeks, although she wrote to him regularly; so, when two of his young friends spoke guardedly of 'taking off', he thought it might not be a bad idea to join them.

Two days later, bending over in the assembly hall to accept his punishment, he reflected it was well worth it: he had seen his mum, she was OK, and so was his home; but he wished that cane didn't sting so much. Punishments may have been severe but there was a lighter side to camp life; in addition to the rambles there were trips on the tractor up the old Roman road, potato picking and harvesting in, as one so often remembers youthful pursuits, glorious sunshine. The concerts and film shows that were put on by the masters and the Christmas parties given by the Portal family, when each boy was presented with a newly minted shilling, riches indeed, in those days.

On fine Saturdays, one could see circles of boys seated in the grassy area which was variously used as barrack square, sports field and grazing space for the animals. Close inspection revealed that the youngsters were being introduced to the intricacies of sock-darning, the male equivalent of the 'sewing bees' which occupied many groups of thrifty ladies in the war years. Freed at last from these unmanly pursuits, the boys indulged themselves in matters dearer to their hearts, crawling through the maze of explorable byways beneath the dormitories and acting out their mock battles before emerging, white-kneed and hungry, to answer the call to dinner.

'Food, while rationed, seemed to be plentiful and substantial,' wrote Barry Little. 'Clear memories emerge of plates of watercress and bowls of honey, although one of the favourite songs of the day would seem to indicate a certain dissatisfaction with the quality and variety of the victuals.' Strains of *There is a happy camp*?

'Yes, they were days of pressure,' he continues, 'although as a child, thank goodness one didn't realise it at the time and I can honestly say that most of the time spent at Lords Field was happy. I remember particularly a member of the domestic staff who, for some reason, took an interest in me; she made sure I did the things I had to do and she almost became a second mother to me. I remember my own mother and herself conferring no doubt about my welfare, when she visited. I wish I could see or contact her again, providing she is still alive, to thank her.

'In spite of the discipline, they were good days, really, and, although some of the boys may have cause to remember some of them with regret, (some of the masters being extremely stern disciplinarians), I firmly believe that the old system was best, even though being in close proximity to the said discipline, one doesn't always think of it in that way at the time.'

Robert Flather of Norwich remembers it and those involved with affection. 'Further, I have always considered myself fortunate in being able to call upon experience and training which in the normal course of events would only have stemmed from being a boarder in a good public school. It is good to know that, in spite of the sites of the headmaster's bungalow and perhaps Nurse Jackson's being all that remains of that excellent school, it will not be forgotten. I was not one of the "escapologists" in fact I was reluctant to leave when called upon to do so.'

Barry, too , recalls, 'I revisited the camp in the last few years and was somewhat saddened by what I saw. Our precious dormies had been partitioned into classrooms and the floors ruined, completely ruined and dull, now definitely lacking that "deep down shine". The final memory of that era is of sitting, in company with a class of small boys, for the scholarship, at that time vested in a certain amount of mystery, like a sacred rite, but felt in some inexplicable way to be a good thing. Three boys were to pass that academic hurdle in 1940 and thus leap out of Overton school destined for grammar schools, among them Taunton School, Southampton, itself evacuated to Bournemouth.

'The three boys were paraded on to the stage of the assembly hall to the unfettered cheers, whistles, catcalls and braying of their brethren; it was oddly reminiscent of the release of a mob of malefactors from a life behind bars; for them, the enforced evacuation was over. They were to leave behind a stock of quicksilver friendships, a piece of their boyhood and a few memories that would surface, at unpredictable intervals, into their old age.'

The scholarship was, in the forties, a more prolonged process of elimination than I believe it is today, comprising then three separate exams. The first of these, in my case, was taken at the age of nine years, when the entire class was given a test to determine which of its members had gleaned sufficient knowledge to merit elevation to the County School. The half dozen or so whose results proved satisfactory were required to attend, with other hopefuls from schools in the area, the afore-mentioned school, where, in our best white blouses, pleated gymslips and black stockings, we sat in awed silence at the high desks, where clipboards supported sheets of foolscap; we gazed out of the tall windows as shafts of May sunlight filtered through the trees until the order was given to commence.

Having successfully solved the mathematical problems, disposed of the English questions and concocted a composition, we were released into the spring sunshine to await the results of our efforts.

I was one of, I believe, three, who were congratulated by our headmistress, Miss Parkinson, and given a card to attend the oral.

On a day in high summer, with white ankle socks substituted for the black stockings, I have vague memories of being interviewed by three middle aged, twin-setted ladies who were seated at an oval table; when I was unable to be more specific than to describe the Weald of Kent as 'a wooded area', I knew from the expressions on their faces as they dismissed me, that this time I would not be successful.

I imagine that, with the exception of the gymslips and black stockings, it was little different for the boys who passed the academic hurdle in 1940. There can be no denying that discipline was strict in those days and obviously some of the masters were heavy-handed in dealing out punishments. Their lives, too, had been disrupted and to maintain an almost constant vigil on their young charges could not have been easy.

They were polite and appreciative of the duties which we performed for their benefit and the discipline imposed was to ensure that the good names of the Southampton schools in general and Lords Field in particular were not brought into disrepute.

As in my own schooldays of roughly the same era, the emphasis was on good manners, a basic knowledge of 'the three Rs', scripture and the arts; all mis-spelt words were re-written until learned. We were allowed to enjoy just being children, but were nevertheless of sufficient maturity to hold down a job at the age of fourteen. Forty-five children comprised the average class; I can distinctly recall how one teacher, striving to keep attendances high, chalked '46' on the black wallboard and heaped praise on the class as a whole for keeping the number consistent throughout the week.

I can also recall the painful memory of a seemingly endless succession of slaps rained on my forearm for no greater crime than talking in class; the teacher, having warned us, pounced on the first girl to make so much as a murmur. One wonders if modern youngsters would indeed benefit from a gradual return to at least some of the old, well-tried methods. Those of my generation were brought up in a world of change. We took for granted the cars and aeroplanes which were in their infancy in our own parents' youth. Born between the wars, when unemployment was rife, we were, as I observed earlier, more or less content with our little lot. Not for us the trips abroad and seemingly inexhaustible supply of pocket money which some of our modern counterparts enjoy.

We savoured to the full our penn'orth of sweets and day trips to neighbouring seaside towns on bank holidays.

One of my earliest memories was of the introduction of school milk for which our parents paid a penny a day, the five pence for the week being collected on Monday mornings by the class teacher. This was later reduced to a halfpenny a day, there being a very real need in some cases of malnutrition.

The milk monitors, before carrying in the crates, would push a hole in each perforated cardboard top, prior to inserting the straws. These tops, covered in raffia, and stitched together by many a dexterous needle-woman, were made into colourful shopping bags, purses and teapot stands. In winter, the crates were placed near to the black stoves which served to supplement the central heating, alongside the wet wellingtons. The milkman who supplied milk for our family's needs and for those of our neighbours had not yet gone over to the more sophisticated method of delivering milk in bottles. His round was a back-breaking grind of pushing a handcart loaded with metal churns, from which he ladled the milk into scalded out jugs with pint or half pint measures which dangled from the sides of the churns.

Only the privileged few who attended private schools enjoyed half-term holidays. For us lesser mortals from the elementary schools, holidays were confined to two weeks at Easter, one at Whitsun, six glorious weeks in summer and two at Christmas.

An added bonus were the days when the school was used as a polling station. At these times many of the children were possessed by something akin to voting fever, when, arms linked, they paraded around the playground chanting:

> Vote, vote for Mr Moore;
> Kick old Astor out the door.

or, conversely,

> Vote, vote for Major Astor
> Kick old Moore out the door

– depending, perhaps on their parents' political persuasions. I privately supported the latter view, for was it not Major Astor to whom we were indebted for our Christmas parties and presents?

In the weeks before Christmas, when rehearsals were in full swing for the school play and the air was filled with the sound of children's voices singing the favourite old traditional carols, we were asked to prepare a list of six items, in order of preference, one of which would be presented by Father Christmas.

In those days, Woolworths was still the store whose proud boast was that they sold 'nothing over sixpence', so we could confidently ask for a box of paints, a rainbow wool knitting set, embroidery silks, a photograph or stamp album, or a pencil box, knowing that one of these, wrapped in colourful Christmas wrapping paper, would hang from or nestle beneath the Christmas tree, often so tall that its top branch bent along the ceiling.

To ensure that there was sufficient festive fare, we were asked to contribute swiss rolls, jellies and bottles of fizzy 'Bing'.

Our mothers, meanwhile, were kept busy creating frilled dresses made from crepe paper, with matching cardboard wings trimmed with shiny tinsel for those of us who were in the play.

We, in our turn, made snowflakes and paperchains from strips of gummed paper to decorate the classrooms and hall.

When the long-awaited day of the party arrived, we hurried home from morning lessons (no school dinners, then) too excited to eat the meal our mothers placed before us. We changed into a party or summer frock, topped by a cardigan, which, pride keeping us warm, as my mother used to say, was usually discarded once away from mother's eye.

Armed with labelled cup and plate, off we'd hurry, for once, to school to find set out on each desk waxed cartons of whisked jelly and plates of huffkins and cakes. Disposing of these and the lemonade and Bing in record time, we gathered in the hall to watch, or participate in, the play, join in singing carols, *Silent Night*, *The Holly and the Ivy* and all the old favourites which have been sung by generation after generation, before returning to the classroom where the tree, presents and red-robed,

87

bewhiskered Father Christmas awaited us.

Then, grasping sticky cups and plates, we streamed into the cloakroom to offer our presents for inspection by the parents who were waiting to escort us home along the sparkling, frosty pavements, where, in lighted bay windows stood Christmas trees, colourful candles, as yet unlit, clamped like sticks of twisted barley sugar among the shiny silver balls and tinsel, sparing hardly a thought for the dedicated teachers who had worked so hard through their own lunch-break to make our special day a success and were now left to create some semblance of order for the morning lessons.

In 1935, we patriotically celebrated the Silver Jubilee of King George the Fifth and Queen Mary, proudly sporting our home-made red, white and blue ribbon rosettes; we felt almost as if there had been a death in our own family when the king died the following year. We assembled in the school hall, the scene of earlier festivities, with the picture of nurse Edith Cavell, a first world war heroine looking gravely down on us; the intermittent screeching came from the saw mill some hundred yards or so away on the banks of the river Dour mingling with the muffled sobs of the more demonstrative pupils. We listened quietly to the memorial service from the Albert Hall, conducted by Sir Kingsley Wood, and joined in as the choir sang *Jerusalem*, one of the late king's favourite pieces of music.

Every year, on 'the eleventh hour of the eleventh day of the eleventh month', we gathered reverently in the same hall and listened to the solemn Remembrance Day broadcast from the Cenotaph in Whitehall. To the assembled children, born some years after the first world war, it had no real relevance but one could not fail to be moved by the sounding of the last post and the ensuing two minutes silence.

Preparations were soon in hand for the coronation of Edward, the popular Prince of Wales, and the shops were full of coronation mugs and souvenirs; but it was not to be and, after his abdication, the souvenirs were sold off cheaply to make way for mugs bearing pictures of his brother, the Duke of York, and his lovely dark haired wife, Elizabeth, who is now, of course, our beloved Queen Mum.

We children thus became the proud owners of three sets of souvenirs in two years.

1937 was a year of celebration. We spent several hours a week practising for the display that we, together with pupils from other schools in the town, were to put on at the local Crabble Athletic Ground.

The infants' school at Barton Road was separated from the big girls by a fence which ran between the two playgrounds. At the age of seven, the girls went to the big girls', and the boys to the boys' school, which was itself separated from the girls' school by the hall, used by both boys and girls, but never, never, at the same time.

Already word-perfect, we sang again and again the words of *Jerusalem* and *The Dover Triumph Song*; the hall was sometimes occupied by the girls and at others by the boys, practising for the visual display, when we were to form, more than three thousand of us all told, the Union Jack, the flag of Saint George, and the culminating point of the display, Dover Castle, complete with turrets and flagpole.

For a few shillings, paid in most cases by a weekly contribution, we were issued with shorts, tee shirts and pointed caps of red, white or blue, and white plimsolls. We had one dress rehearsal on the ground itself, when we joined up with the boys who had been practising, segregated, for the display, and the tableaux made a spectacular sight.

At last the great day, May 12th, dawned. There was no school that day, but I attended a special Coronation Day service at St Andrew's church. The heavens opened, rain flooded down, lightning split the sky and thunder roared; messages were somehow conveyed that the display was off. It was too much, after all the months of preparation.

The display, when it was eventually held the following month was an overwhelming success. A long speech was made by Canon Elnor, some words of which have remained indelibly printed on my mind:

It would not matter how good and wise a king were, if he had not good and wise people to rule over. The children in this display will not be children very long, how splendid it would be if they were to grow up good and wise men and women.

Like so many pixies in our pointed caps, we formed a broad ribbon of red, white and blue on three sides of the ground, then like a living, moving mosaic converged in the centre of the ground, where, still as statues, we formed the tableaux which were viewed by thousands of spectators on the surrounding hills and terraces. Dismissed at last and shivering in the chilly evening breeze, we enjoyed our tea of huffkins, cake and lemonade. Tired but with the satisfaction of a job well done, we went off home with our parents, the singing and music from the bands still ringing in our ears. It was truly a day to remember.

King George the Sixth was a good, wise and compassionate king but soon the storm clouds gathered as they had on the day of his coronation, an omen, perhaps? The children in the display did grow up quickly, too quickly, perhaps, but circumstances demanded it of them.

All our teenage years were spent with wartime austerities. Many died or were injured fighting for our country, many more suffered through air raids, but I am sure I speak for many when I say that times seemed better then, in spite of all the difficulties.

Chapter Seven

NEVER GO BACK

EVERY ONE OF MY GENERATION WILL REMEMBER that we faced the dangers and the shortages fortified with the knowledge that we were fighting, each in our own particular way, to keep our beloved country free and fit for our children and our children's children, to live in. Perhaps it would not be strictly true to say that the younger ones among us were considering the children of the future; we were perhaps more concerned that when the war ended we could sleep with the certain knowledge that everything would still be standing the next morning, that the fruit, cream cakes and other small luxuries that haunted our dreams would no longer vanish, as we woke and reached out, dry mouthed, to touch them, and that all the other things that we had managed without for so long would again be freely available.

Not that we didn't do our fair share of grumbling, a good moan is as much a British institution as our far-famed cup of tea but, as time marches inexorably by, it does seem that some of those children for whose future we were so concerned seem hell-bent on destroying the very environment we sought to preserve.

So many privileges are being abused, schools and youth clubs broken into and even burned down; football hooliganism, which amounts almost to civil war among supporters of opposing teams – this in a country where the Englishman was hitherto renowned for his sportsmanship and sense of fair play, win or lose.

They don't perhaps fully appreciate just how fortunate they are to live in our still beautiful country. Perhaps, in spite of the do-gooders, the spectre of the cane should still loom, with its place in the headmaster's study, a deterrent, used when all else fails.

It seems we really only appreciate things when they are very nearly lost to us – no more so than at Lords Field, which holds so many wartime memories for so many people, some good, some no doubt painful but which, in an age when the government's main concern was for the children on whose survival the future of our country depended, achieved with its many helpers its aim of protecting and moulding hundreds of boys in their formative years into honest, self-reliant citizens.

Many attained the age when they could serve their country in the armed forces or the merchant navy, while the younger ones remained in the beautiful Hampshire countryside for the duration.

Many are still drawn back by names and faces which persist almost as if they could be plucked from the air. Names too numerous to list are recalled. Children, and now grandchildren, are regaled with tales of childhood spent in Overton.

More tangible for me are memories kept green by photos taken with my old box Brownie camera. Mrs Davies and Shaun, various members of staff and three small boys, one an orphan, remembered only as Tommy, perched on top of a haystack with two of my colleagues, Kath and Vera, snapped on one of our summer rambles.

They say you should never go back, that to do so would destroy the illusion cherished and built on over the years. One wonders – do they still build the thatched, rustling haystacks, where bright, beady eyes, ever watchful, note the comings and goings of those who tread the hedge-bordered lane which connects the former camp and village? Do rats still scuttle, straw in mouth, across their path, or has the local pest controller, with all the lethal chemicals of modern science at his disposal ended for ever the remunerative sport of his young predecessors? Do bats still flitter and dive on summer evenings, while girls shriek and cover their hair? Does slow, heavy bovine breathing still pervade the night air, or has the village expanded and encroached on the pastoral landscape?

Do the shining, honey-coloured tables still wait in the classrooms, while chalkdust settles in the initials, surreptitiously carved, stroke by tiny stroke, while 'sir's' gaze was directed elsewhere; and do the transparent-winged, russet-bodied craneflies still hover lazily in the haze?

Is there still a camp or have the last remaining buildings been torn down and replaced by one of those huge, impersonal, stereotyped comprehensive schools, where pupils, seemingly unchecked, wander from class to class, seizing, when inclined, the opportunity of skiving behind a convenient bush until, the coast clear, they indulge in pursuits other than those of the classroom, safe in the knowledge that, in the register, at least, they are deemed to be present?

Would I find, if I returned, no sight or sound of things familiar, trees and grassland sacrificed to the all-devouring motorway, chalky banks screening the verdant landscape?

Surely not; there still must be the sharp turn to the right leading to the pretty cottages of The Lynch, where descendents of the fat toad which defied me to pass him still linger. The river, silted now, perhaps, and not so crystal clear, must still flow, chuckling, through the watercress beds, and hide beneath a ghostly mist behind the oddly shaped trees at Freefolk. Does the folklore persist, or have today's sophisticated youth no time for such imaginings?

I would prefer to think that, conversely, the store has been enriched by tales of those who, strolling quietly in the lanes, insist that boyish voices, imitating the staccato rat-tat-tat of long gone machine-guns and decrying the lack of sugar in their tea, can sometimes still be heard mingling with the birdsong in the spring air; that, by a certain ditch, where long ago three girls examined mud-stained coats, squeals that were not made by bird or rat disturbed the afternoon stillness; that, succumbing to the insistent pleading in their canine friends' brown eyes, certain brave souls who, having forsaken the box in the corner to tread the virgin crispness of the snowy lanes, insist that yelps of mock indignation lingered in the frosty air, not unlike those that were heard as soft, snowy missiles found their mark in a mock battle in recent history. Be that as it may, those who, in their turn, have now become the older inhabitants will, without doubt, have recollections, almost tangible, of hordes of grey-clad youngsters, polite, if noisy in the way that small boys have always been, tirelessly hiking to Whitchurch, emptying the fish fryer's hot, steaming shelves of his mouth-watering wares and, later, when their parents' quite justifiable complaints took effect, their customary Saturday supper, one of the few unrationed commodities, no longer at risk, recall feeling sympathy for them, as, in knee-length shorts, they passed by and glanced longingly at the privileged ones, bearing their fragrant, steaming two penn'orth.

Recall, too, the transcient friendships cultivated with the boys who, in their village outside a village, outnumbered the inhabitants themselves. They may recall, too, their parents understandable annoyance that 'they evacuees' had taken all the best books out of Howard's library, a charge to which I plead guilty, and their perplexity as to what on earth those girls did with all that permanganate of potash they were always buying from the chemist on the corner opposite the Red Lion. At least one lady will treasure memories of the boy she chatted to through the camp fence. Certainly they will know if they read this how grateful we were that, having survived legendary battles long past and perhaps in gratitude at living in so peaceful a village with its main industries, derived from the natural element flowing through its midst, as diverse as growing watercress and watermarking banknotes, they granted us not only the freedom of the village, but in many cases, their homes.

We are eternally in their debt.

May I also express grateful thanks to all the boys and their relatives who gave me so much information and, without whose help, this part of my book could not have been written.

I think this quote says it all:

They were very happy days in retrospect, not always warm, sometimes very cold in winter. Sometimes harsh discipline. Always beautiful in summer. All these facets, coupled with a sense of complete order which, I am sure, prepared us for a more responsible adulthood.

Chapter Eight

GERMANY QUITS, LOCK, STOCK AND BARREL

In September, 1943, after almost three years at Lords Field, I felt that I needed a change. On my visits to Dover, was it my imagination or did my parents really look smaller and thinner as they saw me off at the station?

I gave in my notice with mixed feelings; my stay there had been very happy but most of the long-term staff had left. I said goodbye to my sister and family and walked down the familiar dusty lane past the watercress beds for the last time.

On my return to Dover, I signed on at the Labour Exchange and was given an appointment to see someone who would arrange for me to go to a factory in Enfield, where I would be employed fitting filaments into light bulbs. My mother seemed a little worried at this news but factory workers were thought to earn better wages than most, so I thought it might be a bit of an advantage, money wise.

On turning up for the appointment, however, I was told that as I had been doing domestic work, I could only be considered for employment in a hospital or the NAAFI (Navy, Army and Air Force Institute).

I decided on the former and was sent to St William's Hospital, City Way, Rochester, which was then an isolation hospital.

My duties there were divided between the nurses' home and matron's home, which was precisely the same as my former job in the hospital in Dover, more than three years ago. Also, I would have to man the switchboard, answering the phone and plugging in the appropriate plug, for want of a better word, which put me through to the wards. When worried relatives inquired as to how a certain patient was progressing, I could only say, 'He's had a comfortable night,' or 'She has eaten a little breakfast, today,' and, most frustrating of all, 'He's as well as can be expected.' Sometimes, there would be a slate with the condition of the patients' progress, but callers always wanted more details, which I was unable to supply.

Remembering my first introduction to hospital life, I faced my first meeting with matron with some trepidation but she was the complete opposite of the martinet in Dover.

The nurses, as always, worked hard, but it was their privilege in those days to be waited on at table, which was one of my duties. One day, after clearing the table and bearing a huge oval tray full of dishes, I tripped on the step outside the dining room, resulting in quite a few breakages. It was passed off very lightly. 'Accidents will happen,' said matron.

Cleaning the wards was not one of my duties but I was responsible for keeping the domestic staff's quarters clean, as well as matron's and the nurses'.

I was not really happy there; one of the domestic staff, aged only sixteen, had recently died from rheumatic fever and the other girls kept saying that they half expected to see her there. Working alone in the gloomy corridors, I couldn't help thinking that I might, too. Wages were paid monthly and I had just missed payday; it was three weeks before I received my meagre wage of less than £3. I wandered around with very little to spend, but when I received my wages, I went into Chatham on my half day off, as one of the other girls said that the Crazy Gang were playing at the Empire Theatre in 'Alf's Button'. I thoroughly enjoyed the show, after waiting in a queue for ages. It was thrilling actually to see Flanagan and Allan and the rest of the Gang, whose records were often played on the wireless.

It got dark early and at strategic points in Rochester were soldiers manning smokescreens, which appeared to be drums of burning oil, making accurate bombing of nearby Chatham dockyards difficult. I left at the end of November, with memories of a very cold and gloomy wartime Rochester.

So it was back to the Labour Exchange and a khaki clad lady interviewed me at home for a job in the NAAFI. It was early in December and I made my way, diagonally, up the frozen grassy bank opposite the Plough Inn to Lydden Spout, a hilltop gunsite halfway between Dover and Folkestone. I was issued with a khaki uniform and blue cotton overalls, later exchanged for white when I trained as a cook. Our billet was in former coastguard cottages a short walk from the gunsite battery. On Christmas morning there was a knock on the door

6: The Author in NAAFI uniform, 1944

and deposited on the doorstep were metal tea and coffee pots liberally laced with whisky, left by a thoughtful soldier from the cookhouse. As was usual on Christmas day, officers became waiters to serve the ordinary ranks at dinner, with the time-honoured query when everyone had eaten, 'Any complaints?'

We were cordially invited and, though feeling a trifle bashful, enjoyed a traditional well-cooked meal.

To commence my training as cook, I was sent to another hilltop gunsite, Western Heights, which could be seen on the horizon from the window of my home. On my very first evening there, I was washing up when as usual the ack-ack guns opened up, and bombers began their nightly droning overhead. Suddenly there was a loud crump and what sounded like a firework display to end all firework displays. A bomber had been shot down very close to our canteen. I opened the door, dishcloth in hand and shut it again quickly.

'We can't get out there,' I said, looking at the flames shooting up, only yards away.

'We'll have to,' said a soldier who was on kitchen fatigues and who later married my young instructress.

We all trooped out past the searing heat of the burning plane (thank God it didn't explode) and made our way to the next NAAFI canteen at Grand Shaft. Gunbursts and tracers mingled with the searchlight beams.

On our arrival, we were given tea and shown to beds in a chalk-walled room in the cliffs, with a barred balcony overlooking the dark, leaden sea above the western docks. On the way to Grand Shaft, I realised I was still clutching the dishcloth.

'You'll have to have that framed,' said one of the Grand Shaft girls. One of jerry's shells could land straight in here, I thought, standing on the balcony next morning after a more or less sleepless night. We were told to take the day off and retraced our steps of the previous evening; all that remained of our canteen were burned out stoves, on which stood blackened metal tea and coffee pots.

The sun was shining. It seemed as if we were in another world; below us was a thick cottonwool mist, entirely shrouding the downs and houses below.

On arriving home, I found that my mother had been up all night, dreading what news may have been brought to her. (No telephones for ordinary people in those days.) She had seen the glow of the fire from our window, knowing that I would have been there, and thought the worst. With the destruction of the canteen at Western Heights, we were dispersed to other canteens; I was sent back to Grand Shaft and commenced training with a somewhat older cook.

Grand Shaft barracks were built in Napoleonic times, when there were fears of an invasion by the French, the name deriving from a shaft of three integrated flights of stone spiral steps.

Posted by the entrance was a notice, the gist of which was, 'Officers and their ladies, NCOs and their wives, other ranks and their women' each flight being used by one of these categories. The barracks have now been demolished but the steps remain as a tourist attraction.

One day, the manager, Mr Lee, sent me to a bank in the Market Square with a small case containing the takings of £81, a vast sum of money. Although there was virtually no crime to speak of in those days, I did feel rather vulnerable making my way down the long flight of twisting steps, influenced perhaps by films of robberies I had seen.

Often on reaching the top, red faced and breathless, I would have to pass companies of soldiers drilling on the parade ground, on my way back to the kitchen. Mice seemed to enjoy the free run of the pantry;

often I could see them doing acrobatics along the pipes above the kitchen sink, not only did they nibble their way into the flour sacks that stood on the pantry floor, but I had to sift the flour very thoroughly as it was weevil-infested, too.

On completion of my training, I was sent back to Lydden Spout, having to light the coal-burning range, sometimes with difficulty, before I could start on the mountains of rock cakes, raspberry buns, Eccles cakes, parkin and pies. Luckily, the fire was always well established by the time the canteen opened and I tackled the daunting task of cooking chips to serve with the spam and steak pies, The recipe book had to be strictly adhered to; one day one of the soldiers appeared at the kitchen door with a huge pumpkin.

'Would you make us a pumpkin pie, cookie?' he said.

The manageress was adamant that it couldn't be done, as she couldn't 'price' it, but she must have come to some arrangement in the end and relented, Although I had never even seen a pumpkin before, I managed, with the aid of ginger, spice and lemon essence, to fill three of the large oblong tins with the mixture, which when cooked was voted 'bang on' by the lads. These tins were variously used for steak pies, apple tart and 'Nelson', which was a variation of bread pudding between pastry, referred to as 'sinker' by the lads,

One evening in June, the first doodlebug went over, causing a lot of speculation as to what it might be.

'A cheeky devil showing lights,' according to one fellow.

'A queen bee target plane that's used for practice,' said another. Soon the doodlebugs were to become targets and many were shot down by the battery gunners, much to our discomfort.

At the time of the ill-fated Arnhem landings one was shot down near our billet, causing the ceilings to fall down.

Fortunately, one girl who was at home for the night had a lucky escape, as a heavy lump of plaster landed on her pillow.

We had to sleep on 'biscuits' – straw-filled palliasses on the floor of the canteen, until a nissen hut was left at our disposal. I still recall the horror of knowing that it was on a gunsite and that the gunners were there for the express purpose of destroying the doodlebugs before they reached London. I clung to the edge of my mattress praying for our safety, knowing that the hut was too close for my liking to the grassy mound which housed the magazine. On the very night that we moved back to our repaired billet, the hut was destroyed by a direct hit.

Fortunately it was not occupied. Nor did the magazine go up. I was at Lydden Spout on D-Day and have vivid recollections of a sunny morning, cooking, as usual, and hearing of the landings on the wireless. Some days or weeks later, we walked along to the edge of the cliff and saw a rusting ship lying below; we thought it might have been one of the casualties of the landings, sunk before it got to its destination.

At one time some American soldiers were encamped near the firing range. A doodlebug was shot down among the tents, causing deaths and injuries; our boys opened up the cookhouse during that night and served tea and coffee from gleaming galvanised buckets; we went along to help, and it was terrible to see our allies, half dressed and with clothes in shreds, some bloodstained, streaming into the concrete hut.

One of our staff, Dot, was allowed to have her dog with her, as she didn't want to leave him alone at home; we were all dog-lovers, so nobody objected. Mick, an airedale, gave us advance warning of the approach of planes or doodlebugs, his sensitive ears sensing them from miles off. When he started barking and racing about, we knew, even before the warning klaxon and sirens sounded, that we had to be on the alert.

Often, we were entertained by visiting ENSA companies and many times the klaxon would sound when it was a case of 'everybody out' to man the guns. Our lads formed their own bunch of entertainers, the White Cliff Revels, and held shows in one of the buildings. There were musicians, comedians, a fellow who moved his muscles in time to music, and a tenor, Vin Cardi, who sang songs made popular by the film star Tony Martin – *Tenement Symphony* and *Buddy can you spare a dime*. ENSA was irreverently referred to as 'Every Night Something Awful', but we all enjoyed the concerts, although there was one very large lady soprano, who, clad in a shiny red satin dress, elicited a great deal of mirth when she trilled 'I-I-I have so little to give'. All the artistes worked very hard in their efforts to keep up morale.

I remained at Lydden Spout for a while, then was sent to help out at a NAAFI in Crete Road on the hills overlooking Folkestone. Our billet there was an old dilapidated cottage with no lighting or heating, some distance from the purpose-built modern canteen. Rather than sleep there, we generally made the long trek along the deserted lane to catch the Dover bus near the Valiant Sailor public house, often sheltering in the inadequate doorway as all the hilltop batteries opened fire at planes caught in the searchlight beams. Shortly after my arrival, American soldiers set up camp along the lane, in very cramped conditions.

Arriving back at the canteen after one afternoon off, I went to hang my coat in the staff cloakroom-cum-bathroom, only to retreat hurriedly at the sight of a bare back in the bath. Our very accommodating manageress apparently extended our amenities to the camp's officers!

In the autumn of 1944, I was back again at Lydden Spout and three of our staff, including myself, were posted to St Leonard's in Sussex. There, I had the advantage of cooking by gas, albeit a rather temperamental stove, which blew back one day, singeing my eyebrows.

After a short stay catering for lads from the Parachute Regiment, we were sent on to Bexhill, a little further along the coast.

One of the girls, returning from her halfday off imparted the news that the White Cliff Revels were performing at the De la Warr Pavilion, so that was a 'must' for our respective halfdays.

Usually before going to the De la Warr or to the pictures in Hastings, I would visit Arscotts, a rather select little cafe, where I would order tea, Welsh rarebit and what passed for fancy cakes in those days. We were billeted in a former girls' school, Chartres Towers, which had occupied several of a row of imposing buildings. Here, too, I was privileged to have the use of a gas cooker, which covered half the length of the kitchen and was so high that I had to stand on tiptoe to stir the ever popular chips in the large oval pan.

Our manageress often over-estimated the amount of bread needed; the pantry shelves would be stacked with row upon row of the long loaves we used for spam and jam sandwiches. She would cancel the order for a few days and I would have to soak the loaves in water, and re-bake them. They actually smelled and tasted quite good after my efforts. Any sandwiches that were left over at night were coated in batter and deep-fried next morning; they sold hot for 4d, as opposed to the cost of 2d for the original sandwich. Dried apricots and apples, soaked and made into pies, also went down very well with our customers.

The other buildings in the row were occupied by members of the Royal Berkshires and some Canadians, but early in December a contingent of battle-weary soldiers from the Royal Artillery who had been in the Normandy landings arrived at Chartres Towers; having fought their way through France and Holland, some of their kit was a little the worse for wear.

If the idea was for them to rest and recuperate, the army had a strange way of going about it. They were up before dawn running through the ice and snow clad only in PT kit and heavy army boots.

'Sound like a lot of bloody carthorses,' said one of the girls, peering out of the window as they made their usual run at six in the morning.

The hapless lads were sent on assault courses, then back for more running, in training for yet another tour of duty overseas.

One day a handsome blue-eyed Yorkshire lad from the Artillery was put on kitchen fatigues: 'I'll get you a box to stand on,' he said, observing me, on tiptoe as usual, stirring and peering into the outsize pan to see if the chips were suitably browned. Often we would hear him playing the piano in the canteen.

In due course, Alf, the Yorkshire lad, asked if I would like to go to the pictures on my half-day off. I accepted and, whirlwind courtships being the thing in those days, by March we were engaged, although I didn't get a ring at the time, as someone stole his 'credits' while he slept; he lost the then princely sum of £50 earned the hard way through Normandy and Holland.

On my half days, we went to the pictures or to the White Rock Pavilion where mostly the shows consisted of army bands and talent shows. Sometimes we went to a small canteen run by the Church Army, where tea and toast could be bought for a few pence.

Walking back from the bus at night, we could hear, and sometimes see, waves of aircraft on their way to bomb targets in Germany. The news of allied advances continued and we were all shocked to hear of the terrible scenes as Belsen was liberated.

The morning of Tuesday, May 8th, 1945 was the same as any other as far as I was concerned and, although there was excited speculation that soon it would be all over, there were still the mountains of buns, steak pies and Nelsons, to make for the hungry troops. It was my half-day off, and my husband-to-be and I had arranged to go to the pictures in Hastings. We settled into our shilling seats to watch the film. Suddenly the screen went dark and there were loud cheers and foot tapping from the many servicemen present, who obviously thought there had been a breakdown in the projection room. For a moment there was silence as a hand-written message appeared on the screen, 'Germany Quits, Lock, Stock and Barrel', followed by cheers and khaki berets soaring high in the air. With true British restraint, the initial outburst died down as the audience became engrossed in the film, although excited rumblings persisted for some minutes.

What a lovely feeling it was. No more air raids, no more nights when bombers throbbed menacingly overhead and hopefully a return to a more varied diet, an end to rationing and, lovely thought, bananas and oranges on sale again. Three weeks later we were married in Dover, where there was an almost tangible air of relief. Preparations were afoot for street parties to celebrate the end of hostilities, while huge bonfires were built on the surrounding hills. In our road, as no doubt in many others, raffles were held to raise money and people contributed anything in the way of food that they could. Almost everything was rationed but, on the day, cakes, jellies and sandwiches were laid out on the tables and a neighbour brought round six eggs that my mother had won in the raffle.

The day was rounded off with singing and dancing round the towering bonfire on Whinless Down, where nature had played her part by bringing the hawthorn bushes into full and glorious bloom, while fiery glows could be seen spanning the hills around the entire area as a thankful town celebrated the long-awaited news broadcast on May 8th, 1945. Still to come was the end of the war with Japan, brought to a terrifying finale with the dropping of the atomic bombs. There had been a feeling that we were all in it together but now a new spirit abounded, that of building a bright new future and the prospect of loved ones returning home.

My brother arrived home in the middle of June, with his BEM and a letter from the King regretting that he could not award it to him personally. I had been a little girl of seven when my brother had left to go to India, now, here I was, twenty years of age and a married woman.

Flags were retrieved from drawers, where they had lain since earlier royal celebrations, and a 'welcome home' notice hung on the outside of the house.

Rationing was to go on for some years, not only for food and clothing, but furniture and coal. My mother, too, searched the sweet shops for unrationed sweet cigarettes and gave up her sweet coupons for her grandchildren, as she and my father had given their clothing coupons for my lovely white satin wedding dress and paid a hard-earned £4.10s for it, (£4.50 in today's money).

I remember those far-off days when my entire teenage years were spent in war or the fear of war. We were more likely to be called young ladies, then, as the term teenager had not been integrated into the English language.

I glance at my certificate for 'endurance, courage and devotion to duty . . . during heavy bombardment by cross channel guns in June, 1944, following the invasion of north west Europe' from my days (and nights) in the NAAFI, and I think that, after my husband's demob, when we started a family, my small sons almost believed me when I told them I helped win the war by standing on the cliffs chucking rock buns at the enemy.